Alaska Earthquake 1964
Where were you?

Compiled by   Joy Griffin
Transcribed by   Susie Gibson
Book Design by   Dave Swarthout

Cover by Kevin Hall,
K & H Graphics, Anchorage.
Published by Wizard Works
for the Staff and Friends of the
Homer Public Library
Homer, Alaska
1996

A photograph of the authors is on the rear cover. Not all the authors were able to be present, but those that could were:

Seated, left to right:
Clarence H. "Poopdeck" Platt; Marie C. Doyle; Norman P. Nault, Sr.; Laura A. Hendricks; Conrad Bitter; Margaret Pate; Martine Clayton.

Second row, left to right:
B.B. Talley; Virginia M. Talley; Jan Bunker Needham; Don Ronda; Daisy Lee Bitter; Velma R. Edens; Deborah Poore and McKenzie McCarthy; Al Clayton.

Top row, left to right:
Harold Gnad; Tonda Jandt Alexander; Cathie Booth Ulmer; John Child; Al Greer; Jill Greer; Anne Robinson; Susan Phillips Cushing; Neil McArthur; Joy Griffin.

Not shown:
Findlay Abbott; Caroline Backus Venutti; Fred Carroll; Erma Carroll (deceased); Donald L. Darnell; Dick Edens; Jack Estill; Mary W. Gerken; Roy Hoyt, Jr.; M. Walter Johnson; Patty Jones Williams; Yule Kilcher; Sandy McDaniel; Mary Ann Mullen; Beryl Myhill; Julia Person; Susan Price; Leo Rhode; Patty Shroy; H.A. Thorn; Dianna Tillion; Barbara Tyndall; Aloma White; Judy White-Kruger; Anne Wieland; Charles Williams (deceased); Wilma Williams; Debra Williams.

ISBN 0-9621543-7-7
Wizard Works
• • ♦ • •
Homer Public Library
Homer, Alaska
©1996

The most destructive earthquake to strike Alaska occurred at 5:46 pm on Good Friday, March 27, 1964. Registering between 8.4 and 8.6 on the Richter scale in use at this time, its equivalent moment magnitude has since been revised upward to 9.2, making it the strongest earthquake recorded in North America. The earthquake and seismic waves that followed killed 131 persons, 115 of them Alaskans.
Source: The Alaska Almanac, Alaska Northwest Books.

"I have found these eyewitness accounts of the effects of the 1964 Great Alaskan tsunami to be very important and interesting. They are important to corroborate the extent and degree of damage, death, and destruction in these areas, plus are important for future mitigation of tsunamigenic earthquakes."
Thomas Sokolowski
Chief, Alaska Tsunami Warning Center

Alaska Earthquake 1964
Where were you?

March 27, 1964 started out calm and serene in Southcentral Alaska. People were going about their activities with everyday sameness. Easter was two days away, and they were looking forward to spring.

At 5:36 pm the first rumble came, and, for many, nothing would ever be the same again.

No one who lived through the great earthquake of 1964 would ever forget it. Their memories are as clear as if it had happened yesterday.

In 1994, the 30th anniversary of the quake, the Friends of the Homer Public Library asked residents for recollections of that day.

These are their stories, just as they have told them.

Joy Griffin

Friends of the Homer Library
March, 1996

CONTENTS

Alaska Earthquake 1964
Where were you?

HOMER

Anne B. Robinson
A View From Afar

I WAS LIVING IN MIAMI, FLORIDA, a twenty-nine year-old mother of two infants. We were sitting around the swimming pool at the time someone mentioned there had been a terrible earthquake in Alaska. We agreed that we would rather have hurricanes than earthquakes. I remember thinking at the time how grateful I was that I would never have to worry about such events in my life as no one in their right mind would live in such a godforsaken place.

Homer resident since 1972.

©1994 Anne Robinson

Don Ronda
Earthquake!

WHEN VISITORS FIND OUT that we've lived in Alaska for some time, one of the first questions asked is, "Were you here during the earthquake?" After our answering in the affirmative, the next question is, "What was it like?"

Interesting, to say the least. Not particularly frightening nor amusing ... actually requiring very little of us other than to hang on, observe ... and later on, to wonder.

Our supper was earlier than usual. Schools had recessed at noon because it was Good Friday and I had managed to spend the afternoon at home. My wife, Arlene, stood up to get the dessert from the kitchen counter just as we felt the first jolt. It was 5:36 pm, March 27, 1964.

There was a loud "bang" and the house jerked as if struck by some large object. Our radio, tuned to an Anchorage station, suddenly died and all the house lights went out. "Oh, oh, another earthquake," we thought as the house began to sway with an undulating motion.

We'd been having quite a number of small tremors so we weren't particularly impressed. Earthquakes had become common occurrences in our part of Alaska—in Homer at the end of the Kenai Peninsula. Since they were usually a matter of a few seconds of mild shaking, we expected this one to end momentarily.

Unexpectedly, it continued to build. Arlene was standing with feet apart and hands resting on the kitchen counter when the cupboard door in front of her popped open and cups and glasses spilled out. Incensed that her best crystal was being shattered, she closed the door firmly and continued to hold on.

The house ... was shaking so badly that one could barely stand

The house had begun creaking and complaining loudly and was shaking so badly that one could barely stand. We heard a crash from the bedroom, the living room lamp tipped over, and the electric fan skittered off the refrigerator and onto the stove. This was far worse than anything we'd previously experienced and it didn't seem to be slowing down. If anything, it continued to grow in strength until it could no longer be ignored. We began to roll like a vessel in rough seas. That's when we decided to try and get out.

Ann, our two year old, had climbed out of her high chair and was scrambling across the table to her mother. Arlene caught her just as she reached the table's edge and passed her back to me as we staggered to the front door amidst a cacophony of crashing dishes, tortured lumber, and falling books. The entire house was moving like a ship in a storm.

We bounced off both sides of the doorway, staggered out onto the porch, and held onto each other as we careened down the steps to the walkway out front. Once clear of the building we braced ourselves with widespread feet and interlocking arms as we watched things happen. Muktuk, our husky, whimpered as she cowered between our legs.

The forest around us looked as if it were enveloped in a ground fog as the trees whipped back and forth shedding cataracts of snow from their lower branches. Power lines along the road below bounced and swayed in time with the tremors. Our car, parked about six feet below where we were standing, was leaping and bounding back and forth two or three feet at a time, threatening to roll down the hill. Our neighbor's new house was just across East Hill Road from the end of our driveway so I staggered to the car to set the hand brake as Arlene wrapped an overcoat, collected during the mad dash to the door, around Ann and herself. The motion seemed to go on forever...

After what seemed like an eternity but was actually only about five minutes the shaking slowed and finally faded away. The ensuing silence was broken by the calls of neighbors.

"Mrs. Edens, are you all right?" "How about the Rondas?" "We're fine, but has anyone seen the Johnsons?" And from down the hill, "We're all right down here!" from the Nelsons. All around us people were checking on neighbors to see if all was well.

Living with Kachemak Bay at our doorstep so-to-speak, my first thought was of the possibility of a tsunami or tidal wave. I rushed indoors for my binoculars. We were high enough on the hillside to be far out of the reach of any such wave but an event of that sort would be a once-in-a-lifetime experience. I didn't want to miss it!

The tide was way out and everything appeared perfectly normal when I first looked. Then a black line appeared on the horizon and approached the shore as I continued watching. From my vantage point high on the hill, at least two miles from the shoreline, it looked as if the wave was only three or four feet high as it rolled in and dissipated itself on the tideflats. It was gone before reaching the high water mark and did no damage as far as I could tell. So much for tidal waves!

Then back inside to check for structural damage and help with the cleanup. The power was still off but I flipped the master switch on the meter base just in case. No point in surviving a quake to be burned out by fires caused by electrical damage or broken fuel lines.

A check of the house showed no noticeable structural damage. A check of the wiring and plumbing disclosed no leaks. The chimney pipe was still intact and the oil heater still burning though there was soot on and around the heating stove. The circulating fan was bent and broken and the refrigerator door was wide open, as were all the cupboard doors. Broken glass covered the counters and kitchen floor.

In the bedroom, a glass model case lay smashed on the floor after having fallen off a shelf and bounced off the bed. A glass covered picture lay shattered on the coverlet while books and an alarm clock lay strewn about.

In the bathroom, there was water on the floor around the stool. Toilet articles and medicines filled the sink and were spilled on the floor. The medicine cabinet door was wide open.

It appeared that most of the motion had occurred on a NE–SW axis. All shelves oriented perpendicular to the shake had dumped their contents onto the floor while those along the axis of the of the major movement remained apparently untouched. In spite of the violence and duration of the tremors there were no shattered windows nor obvious structural damages to wall or ceiling surfaces.

We parked Ann on the living room couch as we began the sweep-up of broken glass in the kitchen and elsewhere. Muktuk, still shivering with fear and making a nuisance of herself trying to stay near us, had to be banished to the front porch where she whined and howled forlornly.

As our cleanup proceeded we attributed our silent radio to the fact that power had been shut off. Only when I flipped our house master switch back on did we realize that the radio had been operating on battery power...and it was still silent. This meant that the Anchorage station we'd been listening to must be off the air. Only then did we begin to realize that the quake had been more than just a local event. We tuned up and down the bands searching for an active station. No luck!

Our radio was an Admiral All-World receiver, which could receive all of the various short wave bands as well as the commercial broadcast frequencies. In the Alaskan bush, where we had first acquired ours, such receivers were common. By such means people living at remote sites were able to keep up with the short wave chatter of radio hams and governmental services. It was before the time of citizen's band radios and was the bush equivalent of the old time telephone party line. It proved to be a godsend in our current situation but at first the air waves were ominously silent. All of the Anchorage stations we normally received were blank. Only static came through the ether.

My second worry, as junior-senior high school principal, was for my school. As soon as possible I headed downtown for a checkup. As we drove through the business district we saw no obvious damage. Town seemed, if anything, quieter than usual. We saw few people on the streets and there was very little traffic. Otherwise, everything appeared normal.

At school, the story seemed to be the same. No serious structural damage in either building, but the storerooms and library were a royal mess. Both the library and the main bookroom shelves had been oriented perpendicular to the quake and all the books were in a grand pile on the floor. The shop area was even worse. The paint locker's doors had come open, dumping paints, thinners, solvents, paint removers, and all manner of hazardous liquids onto the floor and the wall opposite. The cabinet in which a year's supply of plaster of Paris, powdered and liquid glues had been stored had then tipped over, spilling its contents into the liquid mess. Storage shelves in the cafeteria kitchen were a similar disaster area with flour and bread slices intermixed with vegetable oils, canned goods, and the contents of a large spice rack. The Home Economics room, surprisingly enough, seemed a model of tidiness. Its shelves had been parallel to the quake.

It was while mopping up at the school that we were favored with the first of many rumors and announcements. A local police officer dropped in to inform us that a seismic sea wave was reportedly on its way and the lower areas of town were being evacuated. Civil Defense, police, and fire department personnel were out in force and encouraging all to head for higher ground.

The school being along the upper edge of the danger zone (about 75 to 100 feet above tidewater), we elected to leave the cleanup until later and wait out further developments at our home on the hill.

A short time later we were joined there by several friends and colleagues whose homes were in the lowlands. All spent the remainder of the evening huddled around our radio by which means we could receive any emergency messages broadcast by the authorities. There was a good bit of excitement in the air as everyone reported on their experiences and current situations but there was also concern and tension which built as we waited out the predicted events.

All the local stations were still off the air. By this time we had found that we could receive KQED in San Francisco so we listened for a while to see if there would be any word on the quake. Two hours after the quake there still hadn't been any announcements from that source. Frustrated with the broadcast channels we shifted to the short wave bands and there we heard our first local transmissions. They were between the Alaska Steamship Line freighter *S.S. Chena* slowly steaming around in Valdez Arm after witnessing the complete destruction of the Valdez waterfront and a tanker just entering Cook Inlet.

The tanker called first, trying to make contact with the Homer Pilot Station. After a couple of unanswered call-ups **Did you say the town is gone...? Yes. Gone.** they were contacted by the captain of the *Chena* who asked who they were and whither bound. The conversation went something like this:

From the *Chena:* "Hey Cap. Where are you located and where are you bound?"

From the *Tanker:* "We're just entering Cook Inlet, abeam the Barrens, bound for the Nikiski Dock."

Chena: "Ah, yah. Better call them and see if they're still there."

Tanker: "Why? We usually just call the Homer Pilot."

Station: "They're apparently not answering just now."

Chena: "There's probably a good reason for that. We've just had an earthquake here that's about wiped Valdez off the map. It may have involved Cook Inlet too."

Tanker: "You say you're in Valdez Arm and the town's been damaged?"

Chena: "Affirmative. It was a major quake. I'm circling in the Arm out in front of where

the town was. I have two dead aboard and
I've just launched the motor lifeboat to go
ashore and see if we can help those poor
devils. There's trash in the water as far as
we can see and the town's about
disappeared."

Tanker: "Did you say the town is gone?"

Chena: "Yes. Gone!"

"We were laying at the city dock. You
know the one with the long pier and the
tee warehouse at the end? Had a crew of
about 30 working cargo and the water
went out and set us on the bottom right at
the dock face. We could see crabs walking
around on the bottom right next to the
ship!"

"When the water came back it came in a
rush. A giant wave washed right over our
main deck and took the warehouse and
dock with it. Wiped all the people away
too. The dock and pier are completely
gone and so is most of the waterfront of
the town. We had three big waves like
that and each one put us hard aground.
Fortunately I had steam up and we were
able to get away and out to where we're
circling now. We're assessing damage
now. Have a lot of water aboard in the
cargo decks and don't know how many
crew are missing or injured. The mate
died of a heart attack and I had one

seaman on the dock that's missing. We're checking for hull damage now."

Tanker: "My God! Sounds like you're lucky to still be afloat. Thanks for the information. We'll give Nikiski a shout."

Next came an eyewitness report of the situation along 4th Avenue in downtown An- chorage. The caller, a ham op- erator, had made repeated at- tempts to contact someone when he was finally answered by another ham in Fairbanks.

We had three big waves like that and each one put us hard aground

The Anchorage operator was calling in the blind, ur- gently requesting a contact from any station. Fairbanks replied in a bored voice asking what was up? Fairbanks sounded somewhat nonplused to be asked to immediately contact the military authorities in Fairbanks and have them send a truck convoy of relief supplies for disaster assistance in the Anchorage area.

Fairbanks: "What happened? Why do you need disaster aid?"

Anchorage: "We just had one hell of an earthquake down here. There's going to be lots of people needing medical help and housing. There's been lots of damage."

Fairbanks: "What kind of damage?"

Anchorage: "How well do you know Anchorage?"

Fairbanks: "Used to live there. Where are you now?"

Anchorage: "D'you know where the Denali Theatre is.... on Fourth Avenue?"

Fairbanks: "Yep."

Anchorage: "Well, I'm in a second floor office
looking out on Fourth Avenue and the
pavement is about at eye level. The
roadway is all busted up and I can see one
of the water mains spraying water all over
the place. This whole building slid about
fifteen feet down the hill toward the
railroad yards. There's busted windows
and debris all around and down the block
I can see several collapsed or badly
damaged buildings...."

"I repeat, this was a major quake. There's
lots of damage and there's bound to be
casualties. People are going to need help.
Major help. Please get the military or the
National Guard up there in gear. I've
been trying for over an hour and haven't
been able to make contact. Our phones
are out and all radio stations are off the
air. I say again, we need immediate help."

This exchange was followed on another frequency by some
conversations between local fishermen as they were fleeing
Kamishak Bay. One boat was arguing that the best course of
action was to get away from shore and further to sea while
another reportedly was heading to Homer to check on
conditions here.

On yet another frequency Civil Defense was on the air
with disaster information, relaying messages from one area
to another and checking on outlying communities that
hadn't yet been heard from. Repeatedly calls went out for

Earthquake!

Seward, a town which seemed to have vanished communications-wise. A series of messages, both pathetic and comical, were from fishing vessels in the Kodiak area. At first there were the calls of boats checking up on one another, each trying to gain some sort of reassurance from the other. Seismic wave warnings were being treated rather calmly as first one and then another vowed to "hang tough and see what's going to happen." A beautiful evening with a flat calm lulled the unwary.

These were followed by a series of calls which remain vivid in our memories. They were part of a conversation between the skipper of a small fishing boat whose name I don't recall (I'll call her the *Mary B* in this narrative) and the *Selief*, a large power scow only recently converted for king crabbing. Both were apparently in the Kodiak small boat harbor. The fisherman was discussing the options with the skipper of the *Selief:*

"*Selief?..Selief?....* This is the *Mary B* calling ... "

Selief:	"What's up Cap?"
Mary B:	"Did'ja hear that they've put out a seismic wave alert for this area?"
Selief:	"Sure did. But that was over an hour ago. Sort of a general alert is all."
Mary B:	"What'd ya make of it? I was thinkin' of gettin' outta here but I don't know where I'd run.
	Seems to me ya could run into trouble just as easy as run away from it."
	"Uh..Are you going to do anything?"
Selief:	"Well Cap, I don't know...."
	"That warning is pretty old... and the

quake was in the Sound. That's a long ways from here and behind a bunch of islands. I'd expect that if that thing got out of the Sound we'd have heard of other places getting hit by now...."

"At least here we're here in protected water. Guess I'll just hang tough here and see what develops. No point in getting in an uproar for nothing. Besides, it'd take me a while to get this thing under way anyway."

Mary B: "Yeah, see what ya mean. If anything was happening we'd have heard...This thing gives me the willies though! Them waves travel a long distance sometimes...."

"Seems awful quiet...Well, guess I'll just stick it out here too. There doesn't seem to be much point in runnin' if ya...JESUS CHR!!....."

The transmission was abruptly cut off! Just a hiss of static came over the air!

There was a long silent spell during which we around the radio held our breath. We knew something must have happened but didn't have a clue as to what had occurred. The *Mary B*'s skipper had really sounded scared as he was cut off in mid sentence.

Finally a plaintive voice interrupted the thudding of our collective heartbeats.

"*Selief...Selief...* this's the fishing vessel *Mary B* calling the *Selief...*"

There was an audible exhalation around our radio. At least someone was back on the air.

"*.... Selief...Selief...*Come in *Selief........*"
"*.... Selief...Selief...*C'mon back *Selief...*"
The tension started to build again as we began pulling for a reply.
"*..... Selief...*This's the *Mary B* calling the *Selief...*"
"*..... Selief...*If you're still on, please reply... "
After a dozen or so such calls, each stretching the tension we were feeling, the gang around our radio broke into cheers when we heard the bored sounding voice of the *Selief's* skipper:

Selief: "Yah Cap...*Selief* here. What's up? Where are you?"

Mary B: "I'm outside the harbor puddling around in a bunch of debris! That damned wave washed me right over the breakwater! Dumped me out here with a bunch of other guys. Some of 'em are gone and a bunch of others are in deep trouble..."

"Man!! There's junk and trash as far as I can see. I just got my engine started and my bilge pump's runnin' full blast. I'm runnin' around in the trash lookin' fer survivors....Good God but that was a wave! I never seen anything like that before!"

"Uh...Are you OK? Where are you?"

Selief: "Just a minute Cap...Let me go out on the wing and take some bearings...."

"Yah, Cap... by dead reckoning we seem to be in a schoolyard a couple a blocks from the harbor. There's a bunch of other

Don Ronda

Fishing boat — Kodiak Harbor   Daisy Lee Bitter

boats with me. Don't know how we got
here but at least we're right side up.
Looks like the waterfront's gone!"
This meant that the 80 foot scow had been lifted completely
out of the harbor, washed over the buildings on frontage
street, and had come to rest about two blocks up the valley
behind the high school. Later on, one of the more famous
pictures of the devastation of the quake in the communities
outside the Anchorage bowl was one showing the *Selief*
stranded with several other vessels at her inland resting
place.

The fishing boat on the other hand had been tossed the
opposite direction by the tidal wave's backwash, out over
the breakwater to be dumped amidst all the flotsam in the
outer bay about a quarter mile from where she'd been
berthed. Talk about power!

Things were pretty quiet around the radio as we continued searching up and down the dial. We couldn't help supposing that something similar had hit Seward earlier, which would explain their ominous silence. They weren't the only ones. Every so often calls would go out to other Prince William Sound or Kodiak Island communities, none of which seemed to be replying.

As fortune would have it the next transmissions we heard were from a ham operator in Seward. His report was serious. Apparently the new railroad dock and roundhouse had been washed away by the tidal wave. The tank farm on the point had been destroyed and the fuel from the ruptured storage facility was on fire. The person reporting said their entire waterfront was gone and railroad cars and fish boats had been washed into the slough at the head of the bay. Many homes and businesses near the beach had been destroyed.

The person broadcasting didn't yet have a casualty count but said that damage was extensive and fatalities were expected.

They'd been out of contact for several hours because their radio station and all telephone communications were out. An emergency communications net was still in the process of being set up.

One after another of the Anchorage Stations began to come back on the air. Gradually an overall picture of what had happened, and what was then happening, began to take shape. Along with this came a dawning realization of just how lucky we in the Homer area had been.

Homer's location had done much to protect us from the serious damage incurred in other coastal cities. Valdez, the center of the quake, lies to our northeast with an enormous land mass between the two cities. Kachemak Bay, along whose shore Homer is built, opens into lower Cook Inlet to the southwest. Any tidal wave from the Valdez area would have to travel along the peninsula's outer coast and double back to hit our shores. The wave I'd seen had been just an immediate local disturbance and not the one which had done the damage elsewhere.

Seward and Kodiak weren't as lucky. Their harbors faced the open ocean, in Kodiak's case in the direction from which the tidal wave would come. What to us was a slightly higher than normal tide, to them was a smashing wall of water which washed out their waterfronts and lower parts of town.

Slightly before midnight we finally realized that the events of the day had concluded. Homer wouldn't be getting another tidal wave. Our radio vigil gradually broke up and everyone departed to spend the rest of the night in their own homes.

During the night occasional aftershocks brought us wide awake. Our husky dog, Muktuk, sleeping on the floor of our bedroom for the first time, crawled onto our bed in a panic when the first one struck. With her every muscle quivering, we didn't have the heart to banish her to the floor for the rest of that long night.

The hours, and days, immediately following the quake were very frustrating for us. We, like most Alaskans, had come through with nothing more than a good shaking. As the events became known and their magnitude realized we began to hear the most fantastic reports being broadcast over the "outside" radio stations. One report, for example, had it that "The small coastal community of Homer...has apparently been completely wiped out with 100% casualties."

Earthquake!

We knew that the damage done to Valdez, Seward, and Kodiak was severe. There were some native communities in the Sound that hadn't yet replied to the numerous attempts to make contact broadcast by the various emergency services, but here in town we were safe and sound. We knew that our families would be doing a lot of unnecessary worrying but getting a message to them had become a real problem. The telephones were out, all radio stations, including our local hams, were swamped with emergency messages, and surface transportation was interrupted by collapsed bridges and/or destroyed roadbeds. We finally decided to send air mail special delivery letters and later found that we had made a wise choice.

In Homer there was very little apparent damage. A couple of shacks collapsed, some cement block walls were damaged, and there were cracks in road surfaces and other indications of ground movement along slopes. Most local damage had occurred in stores and businesses where merchandise and equipment was strewn all over the floor.

The most visible damage was done at the end of our five mile gravel spit which juts out into the bay. There a major portion of our new harbor breakwater had subsided beneath the waves. Pilings and floats were jammed and twisted and the whole facility rendered useless. An exceptionally high tide had flooded over the deck of the ocean dock and marooned those at Land's End and the Salty Dawg. The Spit road had been under water in several places.

The evening of the following day, a Saturday, marked the grand opening of the Porpoise Room, our swank new restaurant just completed at what had been the base of the harbor breakwater.

Arlene and I ventured out for an evening meal. We had no more than been served our dinner when there was a general announcement to the effect that all those who wished to do so should leave immediately for the mainland. The Spit road was reportedly again being flooded by the incoming tide. It was either go now or wait out the tide, a matter of being marooned for several hours. Half of the clientele abruptly abandoned ship while the remainder stuck around for what became an impromptu party.

The corresponding tide of the previous day hadn't flooded the restaurant floor but had reportedly dampened the tires of the vehicles parked out front. This had been considered an aberrant tide caused by the earthquake, something that would correct itself over time. When the problem recurred again and again over the next couple of days it was realized that subsidence of the Spit itself must be involved. Later measurements proved that there had been a general land subsidence in our area. The Homer mainland went down about three feet in elevation while the Spit subsided more than six feet, putting the entire Spit at the mercy of every high tide. The Porpoise Room restaurant, as a result, had one of the shortest runs on record. It opened on Saturday and closed on Sunday, just enough time to schedule "Grand Opening" and "Going Out of Business" parties.

The Porpoise Room ... opened on Saturday and closed on Sunday...

The events of the following week elsewhere in the state were equally interesting to follow. Cut off from the rest of Alaska except by air, we continued to rely on our radio. By the following morning all Anchorage stations were back on the air, their schedules modified to carry emergency communications and directives.

Some were personal messages as families tried to locate missing members who had been separated by the quake. "To the Richardson family, Rick is OK at the West High shelter.

He'll try and get home tonight." "To the Bill Williams family on Oogruk Lane; Your dog is safe at the Jones's. Mary will bring him round when your road opens for travel."

Others were from the various utility managers broadcasting emergency directives regarding their services. "To all families living in the 800 block of Whidby Lane—do not flush toilets or dispose of water in the sewers. There is a major sewer break being repaired at the corner of Whidby and 5th. It is expected that such will be again operable by 4:00 pm today."

Or, "The Anchorage Public Utility District wishes to warn all residents of the Turnagain area to shut off their gas mains at the house tap. Do not light any stoves, furnaces, or water heaters until your service has been checked by an authorized Utility employee."

The Red Cross and Public Health services were providing information about health related matters. "Anchorage residents are warned to boil all drinking water unless your water system has been cleared and approved. Those whose service has been disrupted may pick up water from emergency supplies located in the parking lot at West High School...." etc.

Still others were Civil Defense type notices: "The public is advised that the downtown area of Anchorage between the rail yards and 6th avenue from — to — streets is closed to the general public. Please stay out of this area unless you are an owner or operator of a business located there. This restricted area is being patrolled by the Alaska National Guard and all who wish to enter will be checked for proper identification." Etc...etc...etc.

The messages went on and on, each one important to someone.

Don Ronda

One couldn't help but have a feeling of pride in our fellow Alaskans. We huddled around our radio eavesdropping as gradually each service was restored, as families were reunited, damages repaired. Meanwhile, everyone cooperated and improvised. One couldn't help but have a feeling of pride in our fellow Alaskans.

With unbelievable speed, Anchorage and the other badly damaged communities, aided by the military, worked to restore basic services and a semblance of normalcy. Electricity, water, fuel, food, telephones, sewage, garbage disposal, transport, and housing; all the things an urban area takes for granted had been disrupted. Families had been separated by circumstances, housing and businesses damaged or destroyed, gas lines, waterlines, and sewer lines had been broken, power lines damaged, traffic patterns disrupted.

At the same time, as the damages were totaled and the stories of specific events were revealed, one marveled at the awesome power unleashed by the quake. To our growing amazement however, the casualties, those injured or killed, appeared to be minimal.

❧

In retrospect the quake undoubtedly had a beneficial effect on the Homer area. It provided an infusion of funds for community development which had previously been unavailable.

The entire end of the Spit had to be rebuilt, a new harbor dredged out of its middle, and the land around the harbor and along the roadway raised several feet. This new harbor was several times larger than the original behind the breakwater, and it has since been enlarged several times to provide the economic mainstay for the community. New tourist facilities created an entirely new industry for the area. The funds for these facilities either came from earthquake rebuilding entitlements directly or as a result of projects made feasible by such improvements. Though the Spit itself is much smaller in area due to the ravages of natural erosion, it is far better protected now from mankind's ravages. Much of the vegetation on the Spit is now gone, victim of the encroaching saltwater caused by the land subsidence. That same subsidence necessitated imposition of laws prohibiting gravel extraction from the Spit, without which a local gravel extraction industry would have decimated it. In such manner practices severely detrimental and ecologically damaging have been controlled somewhat by default.

All of which goes to prove the adage that it often takes a lot of shaking to get progress.

So what is our attitude today? How do we feel about living in an earthquake zone?

After the quake there was a modest exodus from Alaska of those who didn't want to ever repeat the experience. We, and others who stayed, considered it a once-in-a-lifetime experience.

We've gone through many quakes since. Each could have developed into a major one, but none have, and we doubt that we'll be around for another of that intensity. Certainly, with the population growth and development that Alaska has experienced in the intervening years we could never expect to come out of another with such slight loss of life.

We have taken what realistic precautions we could regarding structural considerations and site locations and each

Don Ronda

time the rolling begins there's that tingle of apprehension, but it's not enough to really worry about or dwell upon. Our attitude seems to be, what good would the latter really do?

Besides the quakes we've lived through several major volcanic eruptions, a few good storms and other natural aberrations, and the oil spill. All have added a tingle of excitement to life, and most, in the long run, have proven to be beneficial in some way.

How do we feel about living in an earthquake zone? We haven't seen anyplace else we think we'd like any better.

Cathy Ulmer
Sheer Wonder

OUR HOMESTEAD WAS AT THE MOUTH OF THE STARISKI, eight miles north of Anchor Point, fourteen miles south of Ninilchik.
Electricity was new to us on the homestead when the earthquake hit. The light flickered out for the second time as we began to rock and roll. I was baby-sitting my six younger siblings and felt panic as everyone ran off in a different direction. As I stood in the yard in sheer wonder at what I was seeing, the Stariski tower and the trees around me bent so far to and fro the tops of them nearly touched the ground then they swung back the other way so far you'd never believe they wouldn't snap off.

Norma, who was nine at the time, was running down the driveway as fast as her legs would go yet was going nowhere, as if she were on a rolling treadmill.

I stood in the yard in sheer wonder at what I was seeing...

The violent shaking seemed to go on forever! We were all awestruck by the time it was finally over.

It was with total amazement we realized the only mess in the house was the pan of dishwater had landed right side up on the floor and still contained what water hadn't slooshed out!

Unfortunately, my folks did lose a lot of heavy equipment due to the high waves that cleaned the beach off after the ground had settled.

©1994 Cathy Ulmer

27

Beryl Myhill
The Easter Lily

A S I REMEMBER THE DAY, it was overcast and still. Bryan and I had gone into town to do last minute Easter errands, leaving Leon and Loren home with the baby, David. We left a basket at Clemen's Jewelry store, which is now Cups Restaurant, for Juanita to fill with an artificial flower arrangement. We then went to Kachemak Food Cache, now Save-u-More. There we purchased, among other things, an Easter lily. The pot was so broken only the decorative paper around it, held it together. We took the lily to the Assembly of God church, placing it on the alter in front of the pulpit.

"It will be safe there," I told Bryan. "It won't have to be moved until after Easter."

Our errands done, we returned home.

The stretch of road from the junior high school to West Hill Road was so full of potholes it felt like the car had four flat tires. As we drove up the hill, Bryan draped himself over the back of the seat because "I want to know what it's like to go up the hill backwards."

When we reached what is now Myhill Road, I turned into it and stopped.

"Go get the mail," I said to Bryan.

When he got out of the car I thought he was shaking the car but when I looked at him, his eyes were large as saucers.

"There's an earthquake," he said.

"So ... Go on and get the mail," I told him.

Beryl Myhill

The mailbox was across the road so he proceeded to do as I directed. I looked in the rearview mirror and saw him crawling up the side of the road.

"He sure is making a big deal of this," I thought just as a jolt shook the car. "Hmmm," I thought, "the car is on a slant. Another jolt like that and it might tip the car over. I better get out."

So I did, and stood under the power line, behind the car.

"That's odd" I thought, "the power line and poles are swaying back and forth and there is no wind." Just as if power poles swayed when there was a wind! That was when I realized that maybe this wasn't just a little ol' earthquake.

When we reached the house, Leon and Loren had things well in hand. David was okay, Loren had turned off the water and pulled the breaker on the electric box. They apologized because the kitchen floor was littered with glass. Sixteen of my monogrammed glasses had tumbled out of the cupboard, breaking as they hit each other on the floor.

Other damage consisted of a broken water pipe, the Christmas cactus tipped over and the iron fell off the ironing board. We thanked the Lord for His protection.

I called the church to find out how the lily had fared and how they were at the church.

The piano rolled back and forth on the platform but the lily sat perfectly still.

"Oh, the lily is fine," said the pastor's wife, Eunice Lee. "The piano rolled back and forth on the platform but the lily sat perfectly still."

"But how did you reach us? Don't you know the phones are dead?"

I didn't know, for I had called Howard too, and the phone had worked fine.

30

Meanwhile at the drugstore, Howard and Dale were experiencing more severe results of the quake. At that time, the windows in the front of the store were eight feet long, four feet wide, plate glass panels. Dale was standing behind the cash register in front of the windows. When the quake hit, the clerk, Betty Platt, yelled at Dale.

"Get away from those windows."

He tried to walk down the aisle but fell, so crawled about six feet. When the quake was over, a giant wedge of glass had imbedded itself into the decking of the floor where Dale had been standing. Betty was hanging onto a display, of all things, leather billfolds!

In the pharmacy, Howard was standing in the doorway of the office, anxiously watching a gallon jug of muriatic acid doing a balancing act on a piece of shelving that had been dislodged from its original position. Needless to say, when the shaking stopped, Howard grabbed a ladder and removed the jug from its precarious position. No gallon jugs of anything were ever put on the top shelf again, and acids were relegated to the basement.

As the evening wore on, different people stopped by to help. Harry Gregoire found some plywood and covered the broken windows. Ted Wythe stopped and asked if he could help.

"Don't you have any damage at your store?" Howard asked Ted.

Ted looked at him with a sad, sad expression. "Would you believe," he said, "I had just filled a three tiered bin with nuts, bolts, screws, etc. when that quake hit. I can't face that mess tonight."

Ted had a hardware store where NAPA is now. The south end of the store had not been tied into the sides cor-

Beryl Myhill

rectly. One push and the whole south side of the store would have collapsed.

Howard took a shovel and cleared the pharmacy floor of myriad broken bottles and spilled pills. The pharmaceutical companies and other suppliers were generous in their help in getting the store resupplied. Although there was a loss, we praised the Lord no one had been injured. Things could have been so much worse.

Charles Williams
Pie in the Oven

WE WERE ALL AT HOME IN THE LOG CABIN just behind the Parfait Shop which was located across from the high school. There was a fresh pumpkin pie in the oven when the earthquake hit, and it sloshed all over the oven. I had a radio shop in the log cabin. My instruments were stashed on a shelf above the couch, and when the earthquake hit, the instruments started dancing around and attempting to fall off. I smothered them in my arms and held them from falling. The earthquake lasted approximately ten minutes, and as the family exited from the house they saw the trees dancing in a weird dance like a windstorm, except that they were all going in different directions. Some of the trees were bending off to the left and some to the right. The earthquake was very severe. It was hard to stand up and the trees were dancing around a lot.

It was after school was out as the principal of the school and his family were in their home. Their car was parked in **It was hard to stand up and the trees were dancing around a lot.** gear with the brake on, but the car still rolled forward about fifty feet and rolled backward and stopped right where it was before. There was no damage to our house or to our car. The stores downtown lost a lot of glassware off the shelves. There was no radio station at this time and we didn't realize how large the quake was or where it was centered, but we heard shortly that Anchorage was involved and that the road was out. Many of the stores on Fourth

33

Charles Williams

Avenue were sunk down to ceiling level with the street in front.

It was several weeks before we could travel because the road was washed out near Girdwood. Incidentally, the road was washed out on the Spit so that we could only travel to the Spit during the low tide. During the high tide it was closed. I was in the radio business during this time and needed to go work on the boats, so I had to schedule time to go to the Spit during low tide only.

About three hours after the quake we heard that there might be a seismic wave which would come up the valley, up Kachemak Bay. We also heard that Seward was about washed out. Many of the stores were closed there and it was very difficult to get around.

Because of the possibility of a seismic wave in Homer we were told to go up the hill, so we drove up East Hill Road for quite a ways, then waited for several hours until we felt it was safe. The wave never did show up.

My family was highly interested in the earthquake, as I was, too. My home at the homestead was completely fine; nothing was damaged and nothing fell. We had no idea that an earthquake this large would be happening.

©1994 Charles Williams[†]

[†] *Note: Charles Williams has passed away since this was written.*

Margaret Pate
A Crack in the Earth

WHAT A DAY! I will always be glad all four of us were home in the kitchen when the earth began to shake. It would have been very worrisome to not know where members of the family were.

When we began to know, we wanted to get out of the house. The building was shaking so we couldn't get through **... a crack running from north to south coming down the hill** the doors of the kitchen and service porch the first (or second and third) tries. Eventually, though, we all got out into the yard on the east side of the house. I promptly fell down, and John and Mike yanked me to my feet. Patty did a sort of modern dance step and didn't fall. The house animals streaked straight off to the east and were not seen again for hours. The house seemed to dance around on its foundations, but the most frightening thing for me was to see a crack running from north to south coming down the hill straight for the house. It would open a few inches, and then close again, with water spouting up for a couple of feet. I had just seen a foreign movie taken in Italy where a similar situation had taken place, with the earth opening up, water spouting in the air, and buildings, people and animals falling in before the earth closed up again. The crack swerved when it reached the house, going slightly to the east, and then continued down across our street, and the next block. I don't know how far it extended, but it was scary to watch.

When things settled down enough to get back into the house, we found a mess. All the cupboard doors had come open, and condiments, dishes and glasses were smashed all over the kitchen floor. I was particularly unhappy to lose the set of dishes the District Engineer office where John worked had given us for a wedding present. I still have two cups and two saucers though.

Structurally, the house sustained very little damage. We had just moved in November of 1963, and it was very heartening to know it could withstand such a shaking up. We noticed that the house directly west of us on the corner had a great hole in the basement walls, and we could see right through it. Our basement is poured cement, and perhaps for that reason had very little damage. When we were building, John was quite involved with Civil Defense preparations, and had decided to have a well dug in the basement. This had proved very satisfactory; however, the earth movements destroyed it completely. The SBA made immediate loans available to restoration of utilities, and we took advantage of a $1,000 loan to reestablish the well, outside the house this time. John did have to rehang the inside and outside doors but aside from that we had little damage.

One funny incident occurred during all this confusion. We had an insurance executive visiting, but he had elected to stay at the Heady Hotel, rather than with us. His name was Martin Poole, and one of the men from his home office had called and told John that Martin's health was getting a little fragile, and asking him to see that he sort of took it easy when he was visiting, which we translated to mean that a dinner out at the Elks should be about all the entertaining we should do. Well, when the dust settled, John went down to the hotel and picked Martin up, and he sat in our living room worrying about agents he had in Alaska like Pat Williams in Seward, and others in Kodiak and Anchorage, with whom he couldn't get in contact, and of course he was unable to contact his own office. When he demanded a pitcher of martinis, it seemed only logical to provide them.

Our communication continued to be bad. John's sisters in New York state and Indiana could get no information, and my mother in Portland was told that there was nothing from the Kenai Peninsula, inferring that the whole thing had been destroyed. Eventually, after several days, the Red Cross contacted her with news that there was relatively little damage in this location. We never did find out how the Red Cross had managed to get the proper information to her, but were very grateful.

What a day! What a day! Long to be remembered, and hopefully never to be repeated!

Al and Jill Greer
Ground Waves

I HADN'T BEEN HOME FROM MY JOB at the Homer Post Office but a few minutes when I heard a rumbling then things started rattling like dishes and furniture moving. I tried to get out through one door; it wouldn't open. I ran to another one and finally got outside. My husband was in the yard. He tried to walk toward me. The ground was moving like waves on the ocean. Finally, he crawled to me on his hands and knees. We stood together, holding on to keep our balance. We watched our neighbor's house come up off the foundation then settle back down into place. The trees were swaying from one side to the other with such force the tops were touching the ground. At one point we saw the hill behind the Homer Hospital open up a big split down the middle. When it was back together a geyser of water went in the air about two hundred feet. What a sight to behold!

The ground was moving like waves on the ocean.

My husband had moved a mobile home from Anchorage a couple days before the quake hit. They put it on concrete blocks with no mortar as a temporary thing until a more permanent foundation could be built. We rushed down thinking we would find it flat on the ground but, to our surprise, it was still standing on the blocks. Lots of large cracks in the ground.

We were cut off by road and air. When it was all over we realized we had just witnessed an awesome experience.

©1994 Al and Jill Greer

Harold S. Gnad
An Unexpectedly Long Holiday

GOOD FRIDAY, 1964 WAS A SCHOOL HOLIDAY in Anchorage, where I taught crafts at Wendler Junior High School. In Homer, at that time, the holiday was not observed. Ever since I had moved, with my family, to Alaska in 1961, I had been hoping to obtain a teaching position in Homer. So with my wife, Ruth, Peter, our oldest son, and our youngest son, Bruce, I drove to Homer that day to have an interview with Don Ronda, principal of the Homer High School.

The interview having been concluded satisfactorily, I started driving out East End Road to a friend's house, where we were staying. As I approached Rita Walker's house, the car started to behave in a very peculiar manner. It seemed almost as if all four wheels had suddenly become square and the vehicle was pitching and rolling somewhat like a small boat in a very rough choppy sea. I stopped and got out to inspect things and felt the ground shaking violently. To the East about a quarter of a mile I could see the spruce trees waving back and forth like wheat in a wind storm.

Proceeding on toward home, I came to the Walker's driveway and, seeing them in the yard, I turned in to see what was going on. We all agreed that there had been a very strong earthquake. The ground was frozen, with little or no snow on it. There were numerous narrow cracks in the frozen ground and the earth was moving back and forth about a quarter of an inch on each side of those cracks.

When I arrived at our friend's house, I found them trying to get some news on the radio, but all the Anchorage stations were off the air. My friend's wood frame house had suffered no damage, but his garage walls had collapsed, dropping the roof, more or less intact, down on top of everything. The previous fall I had stored my 12-foot fiberglass sailboat, upside down, up on the ceiling joists of that garage. When the roof collapsed, one of the rafters broke a hand sized hole in the bottom of the boat. I was later able to fix it without too much trouble.

As a result of the earthquake, all the bridges along Turnagain Arm, and as far as Kenai Lake, were damaged beyond immediate use. Early the next week I flew to Anchorage in order to report back to work. Upon arriving in Anchorage, I found myself being interviewed by a radio reporter concerning conditions in Homer. I reported upon things, as I knew them, and was able to send a message to my family that I had arrived OK in Anchorage.

The Anchorage schools were closed for a time. I, along with other teachers, was detailed to assist various teachers to clean up the mess in their homes. I worked helping one teacher remove her jumbled belongings from the tenth or eleventh floor of a badly damaged high rise apartment building near Fifteenth Avenue and the park strip. I had to buy another car for transportation because I had been forced to leave my GMC Carryall in Homer.

Our house in Anchorage suffered no damage except some cracks in the basement cement floor slab. Our son John, a high school student, had remained at home that weekend. He had decided to cook a beef roast and was just putting it in the oven when the earthquake struck. He was frightened and concerned because he thought that maybe he had done something wrong and had caused some kind of explosion.

An Unexpectedly Long Holiday

In June, of that year, we were able to drive our second car to Homer and then to drive back with our original vehicle. That June we made our permanent move to Homer.

So ends our story of the Great Alaskan Earthquake of 1964.

Mary Ann Mullen
The Library Bake Sale

I N 1964, BILL OWNED AND OPERATED the garbage business in Homer and was a partner in a new construction business. He sold the garbage business not long after the quake and stayed with construction.

At the time we had been in Alaska 9 years. Gary, our oldest son, was 12 years old; Ronnie was 10½ and Bobby, who was born in the Homer Hospital, was 6 years old. All of our kids still live in Alaska, Gary in Anchorage and the other two here in Homer.

My family lived in Homer, Alaska, on Fairview Ave. It was a dead-end street now known as East Fairview but Main Street didn't exit. I have 3 boys and Bill, my husband.

I had baked cakes and colored eggs all day, so had a large pot of water on the stove to clean up my mess with, as I had running water. The kind you run and fetch. Also, had a bucket of drinking water on the counter. We used coal to heat with, so had a coal stove with a stack robber on the pipe. That's like a second stove on the pipe that circulates the heat normally lost.

It was the first time I had ever had just egg salad sandwiches for supper. That's because I had lots of cracked eggs left from helping the Easter bunny. We were just finishing supper, when the lights went out and everything started shaking. I jumped up and grabbed the wall cabinet door to keep dishes from falling out and leaned on the bottom door to hold it shut. Bill grabbed the other wall cabinet and held it and the bottom one shut. As soon as this shaking started, the door flew open so you could watch my car going back and forth in the driveway. Also watched the dump trucks going the opposite direction on the street in front of the house. I could look out the window above the sink and see the trees bending and rolling around; the ground looked a little like ocean waves.

I thought my car was going to take off down the driveway. It was parked in almost a hole, as we parked it in the same spot and ice, snow, etc. was built up around it. The quake kind of slowed down after what seemed forever. Bill ran to the neighbor's across the road because it looked like smoke coming out and we weren't sure anyone was home. They were and it was only where water splashed on their stove. As Bill came running back, it started shaking harder again and almost threw him to the ground. The kids yelled at him because our heating stove was walking out on the floor and it was just hanging by the pipe. My phonograph started to fall, chest of drawers also, so kids grabbed them and pushed them back. It seemed to last forever. I kept asking Bill when it was going to stop, like he should reach out and turn it off!

When it finally quit, HEA immediately had our lights back on. So we were lucky. The quake lasted 10 minutes, because Bill's watch was the same as our clock, and when the lights went out it quit. When the shaking quit it was 10 minutes later by his watch. We had lots of tremors for days afterwards.

We had a big tidal wave warning, but it came from the wrong direction, so only had high waters. The whole peninsula sank between 5 to 7 feet. The whole Spit changed and dropped. There used to be a "Green Timbers Campground" about halfway to the end of the Spit. There's no longer any dead timbers much less green trees. We had lots of people that night, because we were up high.

46

Another interesting thing was, I had half of a sandwich when the quake started, never found it, so I must have eaten it. Bill found his piece of cake on the floor and his coffee cup almost empty. My water bucket was half empty, also the pot on the stove. My refrigerator, cabinets, and stove were all moved and jammed against the corner wall.

By the way, my bunny and cakes survived and were taken to the library bake sale next day. That was a community function and one of the best bake sales each year.

I don't really want to go through anything like that again, if I can help it, but if it has to be, I'd rather be in Homer. At least there's not as many people, not as many or as tall of buildings.

I'm still here in spite of the earthquake and I guess you could say I'm part of Homer, and it's home. I kind of grew up with Homer I guess. Saw lots of people come and go. Also lots of changes and was involved in a lot of organizations. Also just things going on in general. I've worked in several places, some that aren't here anymore. There's only about 5 years I haven't worked.

Wilma Williams
A Tough Winter

THAT WINTER OF 1963-64 WAS A TOUGH ONE. Work was hard to find. Charlie and I had to really put our heads together to keep the bills paid. The meat from the moose Charlie got that fall saved us food-wise. I waitressed when there was anything available. David was a baby, and cooking for a family of eight kept me busy.

March 27, 1964 had been a busy day as usual. Charlie came in the house in the late afternoon.

"Honey, I'll buy you a cup of tea at the cafe."

I was agreeable and called to Coni who was upstairs in her room.

"Would you watch David and keep an eye on things while I have a cup of tea with Charlie at the cafe?"

"Sure Mom," she answered. "Where are Tam and Terrill?"

"They went down to play with David Hunt. They should be home before long."

Then hand in hand Charlie and I went down the little hill by our house, and across the street to the Family Cafe. Martha Wickersham was in the kitchen, and waved to us through the serving window as we entered. There were several people in the cafe including Martha's son, Jimmy, and his wife, Mary. Their baby, Layne, was in a high chair, squirming and whimpering. I held out my hands to her; she smiled, and held her hands up. I picked her up.

Charlie had ordered our coffee and tea while I was chatting with Jimmy and Mary. I sat down by him at the counter, holding Layne on my lap.

Suddenly there was a deep roaring sound... Martha's teenage daughter Margaret, was waiting tables for her mom. She put a milkshake on the mixer. Suddenly there was a deep roaring sound that increased in intensity until the easy atmosphere of the cafe tensed. The lights went out, and we looked at each other questioningly.

"Margaret, what are you doing with that milkshake machine?" Martha shouted from the kitchen. Margy shrugged, looking a little bewildered.

The door from the street opened: we all looked at Lee Martin as he entered, thinking he might know what was happening.

"I didn't do it." he said in answer to the questioning glances. We all laughed, but it was cut short by the first wave of the 1964 Good Friday earthquake. It shook the cafe until the dishes rattled.

Alaskans are used to earthquakes, and someone called out "Ride 'em cowboy!" Our amused laughter was more subdued this time. Then we got the violent shake that would change many things in our little town forever. Jimmy reached for baby Layne. Sliding off the stool, I touched Charlie's sleeve, and said "Honey, the kids will be scared."

"Right," he answered, and we were on the way home.

His long legs put him out in the lead. I was hurrying but the earth was moving in waves, resembling a big ground swell. I looked up to see two of the light poles tilt first toward each other and then away so violently that the power lines twanged like a guitar string when it is being tuned. I looked back over my shoulder once to see Jimmy and Mary trying to get into their car in the cafe parking lot. They were having trouble because the cars there were jumping about.

A Tough Winter

Charlie already had David in his arms, and Coni and Carmen in tow, coming down from upstairs when I reached the house.

I immediately thought about Tam and Terrill a mile away at a friend's house. Seeing that everyone was okay at home, I ran down the road to find the others. Why do I always forget the car when I get in a hurry? I had no more than gotten to the road when I saw them, running toward home. As I hurried toward them a new wave of tremors rolled beneath our feet. They sat down on the road, trying to hold on, scared to death. I hurried to meet them. When I looked into their frightened little faces, we had to take a minute to hug before we hurried on homeward.

I took hold of their hands and said in my calmest earthquake voice,

"We have sure got a mess to clean up at home," trying to get their mind on something besides our shaky world.

Our problems at the house were superficial; some things had fallen off of the shelves, broken dishes, a container of water spilled on the floor.

We had never taken the house off of the skids, and this may have been beneficial. We had leveled the house, and skirted it with plywood. It had ridden the rolling earth on its sled with no structural damage.

The kids and I went to work picking up, and cleaning up the mess. Tammy was wiping up the water on the floor, and then wiping up her teardrops of fright that fell one by one as she worked. Coni and Carmen were setting the dressers upright upstairs, and I was trying to find all of the pieces to our sunburst design clock when the phone rang. It was my dad. Lydia was upset,

"Could you take Lydia for a quick ride while I get things straightened out here?"

I said okay. Charlie had gone to check on Tommy who was out at Texaco. He also wanted to see what the damage was on the Spit. Daddy suggested I take his new Ford pickup. Lydia and I chatted about the quake, and I turned the radio on to see if we had made the Anchorage news. I got nothing. I started checking wires in under the dashboard, and then the antenna wire. I fussed a little about a brand new pickup having a radio that didn't work. Suddenly a strange sounding transmission came over the radio.

"This is KENI in Anchorage, Alaska. We are on emergency power. There has been a serious earthquake here. Please stay tuned for announcements. We will keep you informed as we get more information." Shortly thereafter they began to give us an idea of how widespread the quake had been. Kodiak, Seward, Cordova and Valdez had all been hit hard. I was amazed. Lydia's reaction to this frightening revelation: "Turn it off. I do not want to know."

I was a bit frustrated at not being able to hear until I got home.

Charlie and my brother, Sonny, had spotted boats that had slipped their moorings and were floating down the bay. They got a skiff and went after them. There was no boat harbor now to put them back into as the whole embankment that had surrounded the harbor had slipped away into a fault that had opened in the sea floor, so they anchored them out. The piling that had held the ramp leaned at precarious angles.

When Charlie came home things had settled down. We discussed where to offer our help. The drug store was selected, and we went to see if they needed our help. Howard and Beryl welcomed us. I helped there off and on for the next three days—washing bottles, shoveling glass into boxes, and putting things back on the shelves. I felt so sorry for the local business people who had taken such a beating.

That evening we stayed up late listening to the tidal wave warnings. My sister, Loma, was dispatcher for the local fire department and had a CB radio. She contacted people across the bay keeping a schedule with them every half hour until, one by one, they had to leave their homes as the water crept up to the equivalent of a 27 foot tide. It was not the tide rising that did the damage. It was when it receded in minutes, sucking everything in its path with it.

It was not until the tides got bigger, in the next few days, that we realized the Spit was never going to be the same. The winter grass that covered the Spit was a thing of the past. People had wintered their horses there since the first settlers had pastured the horses that were used in the construction of the Alaska Railroad.

The green timber area, where the town picnics were held, was another casualty. The Spit had sunk 6 feet, allowing the salty water to kill that fine stand of spruce slowly, but completely. Every building on the Spit needed attention because the high tide now flowed in and out of their doors.

Charlie's brother, Richard, and his wife were in Anchorage, and could not drive their car back to Homer as the bridges were out. Within a week the stores along Cook Inlet felt the pinch because supply trucks were unable to get through. Emergency shipments came in by air. The Homer airport survived the quake well, but the one in Anchorage needed major repairs.

We listened intently to the radio messages from Anchorage for the first couple of days, and then I turned it off. Listening to: "Mrs. Brown is trying to find her five year old daughter Melissa. Last seen in . . .; Mrs. Jones wants her

husband to know that she is at. . . ." It was just too depressing, and it was time to get on with living.
In a few days things settled down. We survived the Great Alaska Earthquake. In my 39 years of living I had never experienced anything like it, and I hoped that I never would again.

Mary (Wickersham) Gerken
At The Family Cafe

IN 1964 I WAS STILL IN HIGH SCHOOL IN HOMER (which was where the current junior high and elementary school is) and was working after school at my mom's restaurant. She, Martha Wickersham, owned The Family Cafe on Pioneer Avenue, next to Hollis's Service Station. The day of the big quake I was on my way to work, but I decided to stop at the Post Office first, which was past the cafe. I was headed down Pioneer Avenue in my mom's '53 Ford, which always seemed to have something wrong with it, when it began to shudder and hop all over the road. My first thought was that the axle was dropping out of the car so I stopped and put the brake on. I was right across from Pioneer Hardware, just past the restaurant about ¼ of a mile. I was worried about the car, but relieved that I was so close to the cafe. I was thinking that I'd better get out and check the wheels because they surely must be coming off from how it felt. That was when I finally noticed what was going on around me.

Out the window I saw the telephone poles thrashing about, going up and down, side to side, almost touching the ground! Then I looked at the ground and it was undulating in great heaves! There were huge gaps in the road and the ditch alongside it that were opening and closing, opening and closing. A pretty big clue that it was an earthquake and that the car wasn't at fault for jumping all over the road! I've always felt that I missed the

... huge gaps in the road ... were opening and closing, opening and closing.

55

earthquake because I spent so much time during it thinking that the car was falling apart.

I immediately started the car, turned around and went back to the restaurant. My brother, Jim Wickersham, was getting into his car and he had a wild look to him with his eyes huge and round. My mom looked shaken too, with great big eyes. She was already in the back of the kitchen area trying to clean up the mess. The quake had done quite a job on our kitchen. It knocked the grease out of the French fryer and slopped it all over the stove and out onto the linoleum floor. The flour from which she made her fantastic pies had been transported out of its bucket and over everything within a radius of several feet. Salad dressings had been thrown off the counter and the hamburger fixings like mayonnaise and pickles were mixed all together on the floor. It was a terrible mess of broken glass, grease and food, and Mom and I were scrambling as fast as we could to get it cleaned up.

My dad, Howard Wickersham, called at that time to say he had a problem at home. All of Mom's Depression glass had broken, along with some of her favorite vases, and the house was a mess. So my mom said, "Mary, everything's going to be okay. Your dad sounds really upset so I'm going to the house. You take care of the restaurant. It's okay, you've done it before and can make hamburgers. Besides, she added, "there probably won't be that many people coming in anyway."

I told her no problem, that I'd keep cleaning up and take care of it. Within five minutes after she'd left three people walked in, then another two. Meanwhile I kept telling myself that I could handle it. They wanted hamburgers and milkshakes I think, simple stuff anyway. But then more people came in and by the time the front part of the restaurant was full (at least four tables) I decided that it was getting to be too much for me. I called home.

"Mom, you got to get down here! These people are starting to order pretty expensive things, and I can't do steaks." She said she'd be right there. She arrived shortly with my two younger sisters, Margaret and Alice, and my dad as back up. It's a good thing she did because we were really, really, busy that night. It seemed like everyone in town showed up for dinner.

The earthquake had occurred about 5:30 on Good Friday, right before Easter Sunday, and had been of such magnitude and duration that people were kind of thinking that this was a sign that the end of the world was near. So all these old geezers in Homer, who would normally never take their families out to dinner, were bringing in their entire households to our restaurant. Then they ordered the very best on the menu. We quickly went through the top of the line dinners, all the best steaks, lobster, king crab, prawns and such. Eventually we stayed open until all we had left were old hot dogs from the back of the freezer, and they were even sold. Although the quake was a disaster for many, for the restaurant it was a boon, and my mom made a lot of money that night!

We didn't close until 3:30 in the morning. The civil defense guy had come by and asked if he could use the restaurant to work out of, since Pioneer Avenue was deemed safe, and my mom said okay. So The Family Cafe was designated the civil defense headquarters. A tsunami was expected to reach Homer around 11 that night. As we all know though, it never appeared.

We were really worried about my two older sisters, Lynda and Jean, who lived in Anchorage. The news we had was that Anchorage had been totally devastated and that thousands of people were dead. All the radio stations were off the air but eventually some ham radio operators got together and started exchanging real information and news about friends and relatives. At some point we learned that my sisters were safe.

On Easter Sunday we all went out to the Spit for dinner. The Porpoise Room had just opened that weekend and Mom had closed the cafe for the holiday. We went out on low tide and Dad figured we'd be able to get back once the high tide went out again. The Spit had dropped several feet due to the quake. While we were out there another tsunami warning was posted due to some aftershocks. The civil defense and police said that everyone had to evacuate the Spit. Even though Homer hadn't had a tsunami after the big quake, just a small surge that might have been part of one, they were still quite concerned. My dad's Chrysler had to get us off the Spit, not an easy task as the water was up to the door handles. When we got to safety we had to wash the car down with fresh water, which we didn't appreciate because we had to use bucket after bucket (no hoses). However, there wasn't a tsunami that day either and just a few aftershocks. We were lucky.

Now that I've moved back to Homer after thirty some years we've made sure to have earthquake insurance—just in case!

Findlay Abbott
Dissolve Like Sugar

I WAS NOT IN ALASKA at the time of the earthquake. I was a freshman at Whitman College in Walla Walla, Washington. Our homestead on Yukon Island suffered damage from the sinking of the land. Using the side of an old barge, I built a bulkhead around our big Witte diesel generator, but it was destroyed the next winter and the generator buried in the beach. We moved our house back fifty feet and it has survived fine. The erosion and change of the beach was a dynamic process which continued for over ten years and resulted in the destruction of much of the archaeological remains known as the "great midden."

My favorite story of the actual earthquake comes from Dick Haltiner, an early fisherman, cannery operator on the Spit, and family friend. The Porpoise Room was a fine restaurant adjacent to the Baycrest Motel near the overlook three miles before town. But the Porpoise Room had burned to the ground and the owner, G.G. Sewell, decided to rebuild on the Spit.

Dick Haltiner was a workman on the project and they were putting the finishing touches on the building for the grand opening. Also, the small

> ... he watched the breakwater "dissolve like sugar into the water"

boat harbor had just been completed with the breakwater approximately where the entrance breakwater is now. Dick was standing in front of the Porpoise Room when the earthquake hit, and he watched the breakwater "dissolve like sugar into the water." The Porpoise Room, with the rest of the Spit, began flooding during subsequent big tides, and Sewell later obtained an earthquake relief loan to build the second story to the building which became the restaurant.

The main lesson we have to learn from the breakwater dissolving into the water concerns the 30-acre fill next to the deep water dock. It is also built of rock and gravel placed on an unstable mud and gravel base. And it has never been tested or settled by a large earthquake. Therefore, I'm sure we can expect that it will be considerably less than thirty acres after the next big quake.

Diana Tillion
Coming Home to Halibut Cove

IN JUNEAU THE LEGISLATIVE SESSION HAD ENDED. Legislators milled about on the second floor of the Capitol Building which held the House and Senate on one end of the hall and the Alaska State Museum on the other end; the marble floors rang with the sound of eager footsteps rushing from room to room doing the things that needed to be done before going home to their districts.

There was a great deal of jostling and laughing, some still debating an issue or congratulating themselves or each other, nostalgic but glad it was over for another year.

The press people moved about through the restless groups, asking questions, digging for motives and results.

"I believe that's an earthquake!" someone said and all chatter stopped long enough to confirm that the building was, indeed, shaking a little.

Less than an hour later the news of the earthquake hit. The ensuing scene was as earthshaking inside the Capitol Building as the tremor that swept out from the epicenter near Anchorage.

The Governor's office on the third floor of the Capitol Building (as deliberately separate from the second floor as two nations) was jammed with members begging news from their area that might come over the Governor's "hotline" telephone.

Anchorage was destroyed, Valdez was destroyed by a tidal wave, no news yet from Kodiak, Homer, and many other areas along the coast.

Frantic legislators from affected districts paced and listened, pale and sweating with the anxiety for events their imaginations made all too clearly possible.

A bureaucrat who lobbied for a social program that might possibly have been useful under this extreme circumstance strutted through the mob reminding the members of the House and Senate how important his program, that they had let die aborning, would now be and "weren't they sorry?"

Representative George Sullivan grabbed the little man by the shirt front and held him, feet dangling against the wall. His glasses flew down the hallway and, while another member retrieved the glasses, Representatives Clem Tillion and Jay Hammond grabbed George's arm that was pulled back to slug the man.

"Never mind your program! My family and other families are up there, somewhere, you damned little wimp. Shut your mouth or I'll shut it for you!"

There were those who wished they'd let George hit the guy.

The local radio announced "All persons living at beach level must move to higher ground; a tidal wave is expected to hit this region at some time tonight."

When Clem got home, our friend Natalie Hewlett had already called to say we could stay with her.

By the next morning, the news reported that the devastation in Anchorage had not been as bad as first believed, although still ravaged by the dropping of the earth, because the clay in the earth's strata had turned to liquid with the prolonged shaking and run off like water, dropping the land above, making holes and cracks that swallowed houses and dropped streets.

The death toll was unknown.

Coming Home to Halibut Cove

Valdez had been destroyed by the tidal wave, Kodiak's devastation was beyond calculation, and the village of Chenega was wiped out entirely, with the survivors being those persons that had gone to the school house on the hill for a school program.

The State Fish and Game radio communication system provided the most comprehensive reporting from areas along the coast.

Clem suggested I fly home to be there in time to do the quarterly report from my postal station that I left under the care of one of the Halibut Cove bachelors, John Byrd.

Driving our car home was going to be an unknown factor and could take longer than anticipated, so we agreed that I would fly home with Martha (age seven) and Vincent (age three) and he would drive with the older children, Will and Marian.

The Juneau airport terminal was jammed with people. No more jolly conversations or recall of the session; the session was a thing of the dim past. What horror waited for them out there at the other end of the flight on the airplane they waited for?

I looked around the terminal. Haunted faces, anxious faces, and grim faces watched the clock, checked their luggage, confirmed their tickets in low voices.

I clutched baby Vincent and pulled Martha close to my side. "Did they say the runway was OK?" I asked.

"I'm sure it must be or they wouldn't be flying," Clem answered.

The flight was uneventful; the land below the same— massive and unyielding it seemed; but now we all knew how vulnerable!

Coming in to land at the Anchorage airport, Martha had been glued to the window, then turned, and with an expression of relief, said "It's OK, Mom, it looks just the same!"

"Look over here, Martha," and I pointed at the tower of the airport on the ground, like a house-of-cards that had collapsed; it lay in a neat pile.

"Oh!" she gasped, eyes round with awe.

We scrambled into a small aircraft to fly to Homer.

At Homer friends drove us to the end of the Spit. The report was that the damage in Homer was spotty; Rearden's piano was reported to have tipped over but a place not too far away had very little happen.

Fortunately, the clay strata under the Homer bench lay at an angle sloping away from the beach, trapping the clay in place if it had become liquid, avoiding the problem Anchorage faced.

However, the whole land mass sank a few feet; the road out Homer Spit was cracked in measured increments. The face of Homer dock was gone entirely. The rock L-shaped revetment that formed a sheltered boat basin on the east side of the end of the Spit was also gone entirely. Left were pilings at weird angles, some with pieces of boat float stuck on top where they had risen above the top of the piling and out of their slot that held them in place. A few boats were still left there tied to whatever was available.

Hugh Watson and Stinky Jones had risked their lives to get out to their boats to take them across the Bay for safer moorage and had kindly towed our boat the *Ram* along; it had been left in the boat basin to have the engine overhauled in our absence.

Hugh described how the boats had rushed out of the boat basin at first, breaking their mooring lines with the force of the flushing motion, and then all came rushing back in again, like a flock of ducks with the flood; repeating the process time and again.

Joel Moss took photographs of the action of the water in Petersen Bay as it receded and flooded over the rocky shore in a matter of minutes.

The wave was reported to have been twenty feet high but came at a low stage of the tide so the possible devastation was greatly reduced.

Our neighbor, Tom Larson, came to pick the children and me up in our big green skiff.

In Halibut Cove I was shocked to see our dock sticking up into the air, pilings dangling down; as if

... to see our dock sticking up into the air, pilings dangling down

some giant had lifted the end of it out of the mud. The level of the water was evident along the wall of the warehouse with a dry mud line sprinkled with debris just below the windows.

"Don't worry," Tom said cheerfully, "we picked all the motors and things that would be hurt by the water and set them as high as we could," at my look of horror.

"We knew there'd be a wave, so we just went around and set things up," he said as matter of factly as if it happened once a week.

I couldn't help smiling, "I suppose you read and drank coffee through the whole thing." I said.

He looked at me startled, knowing I was chiding him. "Well, it was just an earthquake! We have lots of those!"

"Say," he said, changing the subject, " I need a hair cut; we all need a hair cut; do you think you could cut our hair this afternoon? The house is warm, I built the fire for you."

How could it be? It was as if I had never left, the earthquake had never happened, anxiety didn't exist!

Diana Tillion

"Sure," I said, depositing Vincent in the house. "Sure, Tom, come on over later."

Elmer brought beer, (his home brew; he considered it superior to Rosenblad's) and while I cut hair each one told their version of the earthquake—several times!

Fred Carroll
A Husband's View

WE WAS JUST ABOUT READY TO EAT DINNER when the earthquake hit, and it didn't do any damage to us except it tipped the bird cage over and broke glass out of one side of it. Erma was standing there holding the bird cage. When I got up she thought I was going outside. She said, "Don't you go outside and leave me in here." I wasn't going outside. I just got up to move over a little bit. While I was up, I stomped my foot and said, "Stop!" And about that time this earthquake stopped. To assess our damage, why I think maybe we had one jar of jam fall off the counter here. The trees looked like they were going to fall over, and the house looked like it was doing the watusi or something like that. We didn't lose a window pane or anything.

After it quit, Erma put the dinner on and about that time Larry Farnen called up and he says, "What the heck is Fred doing?" Erma says, "He's eating dinner." "Eating dinner? Tell him to get himself down here to this power plant." At that time we were generating our own power down there. I don't know who was on shift at that time. Maybe nobody was on there. I finished eating dinner. Then I went on down to the plant and about the only thing wrong down there was we had little 75 kw generators that we want to use when the load was bigger than what 300 and 600's that we had in there. Anyway, one of the panels that you control those with was tipped over. Otherwise there was nothing wrong down there. Homer never did lose power. Everybody had power here as far as I know.

Fred Carroll

During the earthquake the Spit dropped 6 feet. Well, the whole area, this whole country around here, dropped 6 feet. Water came in over the Spit road out there and it was actually kind of a mess around here. Nobody lost their lives. I guess maybe some of the stores over there had quite a little stuff drop off the shelves and get busted, something like that, but otherwise I think Homer was real lucky during that earthquake. By the way, the late Larry Farnen was the manager of the Homer Electric Association at that time.

Erma J. Carroll
A Wife's View

Old Home Town
(shook up but here!)
March 30, 1964
Dear Bill and Gloria,[†]
   Got set to write you a line this evening but had company
and they just left. We came through the shake OK with no
damage to us or to the house. Not a window cracked but I'll
never know why. The darn thing shook for 4 minutes. We
lost something like $25.00 worth of dishes, etc. I have fewer
plants to water now and what a mixture of honey, jelly, and
broken glass on the floor. We were very lucky. I don't know
why that every structure here didn't collapse. Had this been
a city the size of Anchorage things here would have been a
mess, too.
   The heaviest damage here was on the Spit. The end of
the Spit is some 4 feet or so lower than before. Water went
into the floor of the Land's End. Also onto the floor of the
new Porpoise Room by the small boat harbor. The sea wall
of the small boat harbor on the side sunk. There is little of it
left. There is supposed to be 210 fathoms of water there
now. The pilings are all leaning. The H.E.A. went down today and removed the lights. We are having high tides now
and they are much higher than they should be. Today's tide
should have been 18 feet and it was 22 feet. We had no tidal
wave or if there was it was a darn small one.

[†] My son and daughter-in-law

Erma J. Carroll

A few chimneys shook down and heard one house had been condemned, don't know where. There are cracks down on the Spit, not wide, six inches some of them perhaps, and a number of cracks across the road by Beluga Lake. Homer was just lucky. A lot of small villages on Kodiak Island are either wiped out or practically so. Myrle and family are OK and guess their house is too. They sent a message to Nola; there are sixteen concrete bridges between Anchorage and Seward gone. What a mess! You are probably getting as much news about it as we are.

Did you have much of a shake in Fairbanks? We heard that you didn't. Write and let us know what happened there and how you are etc. I am listening to the radio, talking to Fred and trying to write so guess I'll give it all up and go to bed. Hope we get through the night without shakes. We are still having aftershocks and some of them are quite sharp. The last one [was] early this morning. The grocery, drug and liquor stores and also the bars lost a lot of stock. The windows are broken out of the drug store.

Love to all,
Mom

©1994 Erma J. Carroll

Erma J. Carroll
Aftermath

Homer, Alaska
April 2, 1964
Dear Gertrude,

Received your letter today, have been intending to write to you all week. This has been rather a busy week. We came thru the "Big Shake" in good condition. The house was not damaged although I don't know why it didn't collapse. Not even the windows cracked. We had approximately $25.00 in broken dishes, etc.

It was quite an experience and I certainly hope we never have another one like it. The shaking lasted four minutes. Homer was very lucky. The damage here was negligible here as compared with other places. Most of the damage was to the small boat harbor and the Spit. It seems to have sunk a few feet and may be still going down. I will send you a couple of clippings from one of our local papers. I was just about to put dinner on the table when it started to shake.

At first we thought it was just an ordinary little quake, but soon had reason to change our minds. What a mess on the kitchen floor when it was all over. A mixture of jelly, honey, broken glass, and at the last, a jar of peanut butter that decided to join the rest of the mess on the floor. In the bathroom everything fell out of the medicine cabinet into the wash bowl.

Some report a tidal wave here. If there was one, it was a very small one, although the tides did act most peculiar. After the quake it would go out a few feet and then come back in again. We did go to higher ground just in case. There were all kind of reports coming in. One said there was a tidal wave of 70 ft. about to hit Homer, (I had my boots and coat ready on that one) then another report said it was only a 15 ft. wave and I knew that wouldn't do us any damage. Then we heard a 50 ft. wave had hit Kodiak so we took a ride up on the hill. The tidal waves were what did most of the damage to Kodiak, Valdez and Seward. We knew a teacher in Valdez who was lost on the dock with his two little boys. He was our neighbor in Fairbanks when he was a kid.

It is a terrible thing, but don't believe all you hear in the news. The people killed isn't nearly as many as they have been reporting in the papers in the States. For instance, they reported Homer had been completely demolished and washed away by a tidal wave. Another report said three were killed here. None were even scratched. The family in Fairbanks was all excited but we couldn't call them. I wrote to them, they must have the letters by now.

It is unbelievable how fast a recovery Anchorage is making. All the radio stations were knocked out but one was back on the air in a very short time. There are still a lot of people missing but many that were missing are all right. Some of these small native villages are hard to check on. I expect the loss of life in some of them must have been heavy. I guess we'll dig out from under the mess in due time. People in Anchorage and the other towns are all ready planning to build again.

We had our biggest snow storm of the year just before this quake. I am glad that it didn't happen about three weeks ago. They were having some sub-zero weather in Anchorage. We haven't had many moose around this winter. I don't believe there was enough snow in the hills to bring them down.

I've been doing quite a lot of knitting this winter. Also made myself a dress. It turned out rather nice, I'm really pleased with it.

We've had a lot of icy roads this winter. I got so I could do fairly well in my little ole jeep on the ice. When it was too slick I just put "Bouncing Belle" into four wheel drive and she behaved herself fairly well.

Fred is down bowling tonight. Our League is over. Didn't do so well this year My progress was all in reverse. I started out with a 132 average and ended up with a 127.

We didn't do anything Easter but listen to the news reports of the quake. Don't worry about your hat and coat. A hat I don't have, and I can't remember when I bought my coat. It's too long. I didn't shorten it because I've been hoping these blasted skirts would get longer but guess they aren't going to. Expect I'll come to it and shorten it yet. When I do just watch'em go down!

Your Easter dinner sounds mighty good. Bet it tasted as good as it sounds.

We're still getting the "Down East" magazine. It is a beautiful little magazine. We also still subscribe to the "Yankee." Thanks for renewing our subscription to "Down East."

We have a little wild bird that lost its wing at the joint. It's a little cross-bill. Did you ever see one? It's beak is quite long and crosses at the end. It's a little curved. Their choice item of food is spruce cones. We thought it was a boy so Fred named it Confucius. We find that it is a girl bird so now we call him, her I mean, Madam Confucius. We've had it about a month now. It's doing fine. It also eats seeds along with the cones.

Erma J. Carroll

I'd send you some pictures of the quake but expect you'll soon be getting them in the papers out there. These clippings aren't much but will give you some idea. Can't think of any more chatter so will close. Write again soon.

Love as ever,
Erma[†]

[†] *Note: Erma Carroll has passed away since this was written.*

74

Velma R. Edens
Everything Was in Shambles

AFTER SLIPPING A ROASTER PAN of Dick's favorite meal of moose roast with vegetables in the oven, I set out to decorate six dozen Easter cookies for the Homer Library Easter Bake Sale to take place the next day. The sugar cookies in shapes of little chicks, rabbits, eggs, crosses, flowers, etc., were prettily done and exhibited fine details. Those little eyes and whiskers looked so realistic. I was sure they'd sell well at the sale, and my boys agreed. However, they talked me into setting aside a few for dessert that night of March 27th.

The boys were more than happy to help me set the table for supper. There in the middle set the plate of tempting cookies. All the others were lying flat, side by side, on the counter to dry the frosting a bit more and to be sorted and packaged later.

I looked out the window and saw the tall spruce trees swaying back and forth, then bowing forward like an Oriental greeting

I was getting ready to put away the frosting ingredients, decorating supplies, and dirty dishes and cookie sheets, etc. when I felt the shaking begin. Suddenly what was light became intense.

I called my three sons from where they were playing and we huddled closely on the couch. Realizing we were sitting under a light fixture, and next to a sheephead mount and large window, I wanted to get us onto the floor so we could

Velma R. Edens

crawl over to be under the table. But as hard as we tried, we couldn't move at all.

I wondered when the shaking was going to stop. I looked out the window and saw the tall spruce trees swaying back and forth, then bowing forward like an Oriental greeting. The lawn appeared like rolling waves and really disturbed our dog, for he too knew something dreadful was going on.

It was frightening to be there and watching all those cookies and baking supplies and utensils flying all over and hitting the floor. Only two or three cookies weren't broken into crumbs! Many dishes, glassware, flavorings and spice cans fell on top of everything. Everything was in shambles with the kitchen cupboards spilling out their contents.

The boys and I prayed together that the quake would stop and that daddy would be safe and able to drive home. I had envisioned the road cracking open somewhere enroute perhaps making his home-coming a great delay. But before long, he drove into the driveway and bounded into the house to see if we were all safe and together.

His eyes could hardly believe the mess. Assessing the grocery room, he found it 3 feet deep with canned goods. He threw cans to the back, one can at a time, and eventually was able to open the door inwardly.

I had watched his sheephead mount roll in two complete circles before it came to rest upside down on the wall. He straightened it back in place. He helped in cleaning up the debris.

We were thankful the oven door hadn't opened. We were among the few in Homer who were able to eat a hot meal fairly soon.

Dick and Brant met after supper to remove the 6x truck from the draw into which it had slid out of sight. And, the

76

boys and I talked the rest of the evening about what an eventful day it had been.

I sent a message via Red Cross that never reached my folks in Portland, Oregon. They had heard via TV news that Homer was "wiped off the map." Imagine their fearing the worst! We were later able to have our ham-operator friend contact my brother-in-law, Clark Calkins, in Portland, to relay the message we were okay. This was comforting for the family to know for certain.

I can't feel a tremor to this day but that I recall the BIG ONE in 1964! Nor can I think of Good Friday, Easter Day or Easter Bake sales.

The Edens families had just been brought their meal at the Porpoise Room out on the Spit Easter Day when we were informed a tsunami wave was expected to hit and cover the Spit, and we had to be evacuated immediately. There wasn't a formal evacuation plan for driving off the Spit, but we were gone and off of there in record time, in spite of driving through some deep water in places. Am so glad we didn't stall. We went elsewhere and reordered our meal and called it a day—a very unusual Easter Day.

©1994 Velma R. Edens

Dick Edens
More Than A Tremor

L ET ME TELL YOU ABOUT MY EXPERIENCE with the big earthquake.[†] To start with, before the earthquake even happened, I got a phone call from Brant, my brother and business partner, saying the old 6x truck having a snowblade on front had gotten stuck alongside a good-sized draw. We would be closer to getting it out of this predicament if my supper, unlike his, wasn't ready and I could run down to our shop for some chains. I hurriedly left for town.

I unlocked the door and ran inside; and just as I was stooping down to pick up the chains, I felt a tremor and things began shaking. I didn't think about it much at first as we're used to having little shakes quite frequently. However, before I hardly straightened up, I decided it was more than just a little tremor. Pretty quick things started falling all around me. The lumber we had hung up on beams, the tools and crankshaft we had on the bench, and a few other odds and ends started flying all around me. So I decided it was a good place in which to leave. I had had the engine out of my car. It was setting on the shop floor and jumping up and down, and the car was jumping violently like a jumping jack. I don't know how I had run out of the shop; because after I got outside, I couldn't stand up at all and had to get down on my knees.

[†] As told by Dick Edens, Nov. 1964. Submitted by Velma R. Edens

The trees weren't swaying way over like they did in many places, as described to me later, but they were quivering just as if a whip was out there jiggling. The trucks were swaying back and forth and jumping up and down and appeared like they were moving at least 10 to 15 feet. After it was all over and the mess was starting to straighten out, I checked it out and actually observed they had moved only about 8 to 10 inches. The truck-track marks showed that the ground was moving like that.

After I got outside I didn't know if I should be there or whether I should go back inside the shop. Either way, it was really bad. I was sure the shop was going to fall down because it looked like a piece of spaghetti going all over the place.

Words cannot describe the breaking and crashing sounds of the windows of the Vern Mutch Drug Store, and those of the propane gas bottles clanging against one another and falling from the porch of Tom Shelford's propane shop next door. They were so loud and deafening. This was a serious situation.

Just as soon as the earthquake quit shaking, I jumped into the pickup and headed home for I was sure Velma would be scared, and I was right! When I walked into the door, I could see there was hardly an inch of the floor that didn't have something laying on it. Dishes and odds and ends were everywhere. The grocery room was 3 feet deep with canned goods. Luckily it didn't hurt the house any.

After seeing the family was fine, Brant and I were ready to head for the 6x truck. We spent a good while getting it out. It hadn't tipped over, but it was clear out of sight in the draw and couldn't be seen from the road.

You wouldn't recognize the Spit any more since the earthquake! The whole thing has changed completely. The

Standard Oil Terminal   Dick Edens

small boat harbor sank, and all that was left was about 100 feet of the outside jetty. Where it left the shore before, it's now going to be part of the entrance to the new boat harbor. It will go toward Homer in the form of a "U." They are putting the main basin clear inside the Spit now which is going to be 10 acres big and will be dug out to minus 14 feet. They hope to have the excavating done by the middle of January, 1965. It will offer a lot of protection none of the boats presently have, and will help the fishermen considerably. We are getting a new dock which is about one-third completed. We're hoping it will be big enough that the big Sealand Transportation Company out of Seattle can land their big ships here. That will give us lower freight rates, hopefully.

The Standard Oil tanks sank considerably and were getting as much as 6 feet of water on them. They've all been raised now. We've had a new fill-stand and pump house installed. Makes it much nicer for us in loading the fuel tanker trucks. In fact, we can load in ten minutes where we were taking twenty to thirty minutes to get loaded sometimes and didn't always get what we wanted either.

The whole end of the Spit has become considerably shorter than it used to be due to the fact that it is sunken. In building it back up, the high tides have pushed the beach 150 to 200 feet from where the old Salty Dawg was.

The tides have been pretty rough out where Lee Shelford's cannery was. It's still there but he's been asked to move his cannery and set it up in a little different position. They are planning to fill in that area, and then he hopes to plan to build a brand new cannery.

Every time there is a high tide, the road to the Spit just about goes completely under water one to six feet deep. If we get the wrong kind of storm on these really high tides which are about 20 to 20½ ft., we probably won't have a road out there at all. It gets covered with driftwood, sand, and all kinds of debris every time it gets over a 19 ft. tide. The road is supposed to be built up this coming summer. Anyway, we hope it is. The latest word is that it's going to be built to a 29 foot level from the low water. The gravel they are going to use to build it up will come from the north end of the harbor. It's estimated that it will put it around 1000 to 1200 feet longer.

I started commercial fishing the first of July. Had a pretty fair season. The whole country where we generally fish sank quite a bit in the earthquake. It was a lot tougher fishing in close to shore. This year I put on extra depth of gear. It paid off well for the deeper fishing all right; but when we got anywhere near the shore, we kept hanging up, which caused us to tear up a lot of gear. Along towards the end of the fishing, I had to take the net ashore and chop the extra off.

Some of the channels changed in a good bit of the country where the rivers got hit by the tidal waves. Where we used to be able to run the boat up to half a mile up the river to see where the fish were spawning, you could run the boat up into the timber! In fact, I took the *Lowan* so far up the mast was hanging up in the trees, so had to turn around. Course, there were a lot of bear feeding on the fish up in there. Enjoyed strolling up and down the river several times. One time in crossing a log, I stepped onto the other side only to slide on a rock and fell in. My, but that water sure was cold! I needed a bath all right, but I wasn't looking for one in this way, however.

We fished in the Nuka Bay area some too. Down in that country, the whole coastline sunk very erratically. Some of it from 4 to 20 feet. In a lot of places one could see only the tops of spruce trees sticking out of the water. A lot of the rocks that used to be out at high water or half-tide were completely out of sight and were a menace to fishing. I barely missed a real jagged one. Had I hit it, it would be the end of the *Lowan* because it was three-quarters loaded with fish. Had a good crew with me this year, and we all got along fine.

Through it all, Alaskans pulled together and grew stronger to rebuild in their time of loss.

Leo Rhode
City Problems

ON MARCH 27, 1964 SHORTLY AFTER 5:00 PM an earthquake measuring 8.9 on the Richter scale hit Homer. On my way home from work, I had just driven into the driveway of my home on Kachemak Drive when the quake hit the area. The ground shook so violently I could not get out of my car to open the moose gate that served as protection for the small trees and shrubs which had been planted in prior years. At the time my wife, Floris, was visiting a neighbor, Hulda Nelson, who lived some two miles away. Neither she nor the neighbor were injured.

Our house was not damaged; however, the land mass dropped some two feet in the area, causing some high tide erosion in areas of Kachemak Bay. Our property, presently owned by Dr. Paul and Frankie Sayer, had a minimum of beach erosion.

In the town proper there was little physical damage. The major loss was in the grocery stores where shelf goods were dumped onto the floors.

The people of Homer had, prior to the quake, voted to become a first-class city. However, the court system had not verified the election by the time of the quake, but did so on March 31, 1964. At that time Homer did not have a water or sewer system. Residences, at the time, built and maintained their own individual systems.

After the quake some water wells lost their capacity and some became questionable in purity.

It was in 1964, after the earthquake, that Homer created its original water system. The sewer system was built in

Leo Rhode

1970. Homer was supplied with electric power by the Homer Electric Association Inc., with whom I was employed as Account and Staff Assistant at the time. At the time of the quake there was a power outage of only 5 to 17 minutes depending on where you lived.

The major damage caused by the quake was on the Homer Spit. The Spit dropped, according to reports, from 3 feet at the take off to 11 feet on the end of the Spit proper. On high tides the road was not useable and Land's End Resort was confronted with 2 feet of water in the dining room at the time of high tides.

The rock wall protecting the boat harbor entrance and its northeast side completely disappeared, reported to have dropped some 60 feet. The harbor was no longer protected thus creating the necessity of building a new facility.

All oil tanks on the end of the Spit were raised and the Salty Dawg Saloon was moved to its present location, as was the original Porpoise Room building which is presently used as the maintenance headquarters by the City.

Tonda Jandt Alexander
A Child's Story

I WAS 9 YEARS OLD, ALMOST 10, during the 1964 earthquake. Because it scared me so bad, I think I've blocked some of it out. But I do remember a few incidents and know others because of hearing them told again and again.

About 15 minutes before the earthquake started, the dogs began howling and ran under the house. The cows ran in from the pasture and were running around as if being bitten by flies or stung by a bee.

About 15 minutes before the earthquake started, the dogs began howling and ran under the house.

About that time my father, Kenney Jandt, left to get some water in Anchor Point, as we didn't have running water. He made it as far as one mile south of Anchor Point, in front of the log home where Baldridges used to live.

At first he thought he had a flat tire and began to slow down. Then the car was shaking so badly he thought he had two flat tires. He almost ripped out the transmission trying to slow the car down and stop. At that time he noticed the road cracking open and the trees swaying so badly that the tops of some came close to touching the ground. Getting out of the car my dad found he couldn't stand up without hanging onto something.

The grandmother and children at the log house came running outside screaming. My dad tried to calm her down.

Tonda Jandt Alexander

The rest of us were at home. We had a lady living with us who was so scared she downed a jug of vodka in a short period of time.

We had a tractor sitting in the yard that was so frozen in the ice, my dad hadn't been able to get it out. The earthquake knocked it right out of there. Also, a barrel we collected water in was almost empty by the end of the earthquake. It had been full. Things fell all over in the house but the house held up.

We packed a few things and took sleeping bags and went over to Sims who owned the Gusher Bar on the Old Sterling Highway in order to be near a phone. I don't believe we stayed there though.

Over the next several days there were many aftershocks and I begged my dad to get us to an airplane because in the air we wouldn't have to feel any earthquakes.

To this day if an earthquake hits I jump up and down so as not to feel the earthquake so well.

Jack Estill
A View of the Spit

THIS ACCOUNT OF MY EXPERIENCE in the great quake of 1964 is dredged up from a mind which has since seen thirty years of life. Some of my recollections may not be sequentially accurate but my memory of the earthquake moments are clearly and indelibly etched in bold print on my conscious mind. I grew up in Southern California and had experienced many earthquakes in my life. Indeed, I had been shaken off my feet before. I never thought much of it and didn't worry about such momentary things. This earthquake shook my confidence in terra firma and disillusioned me to the bone! I'm glad I was there, but let me tell you, there is no terror like not knowing.

My first thought was of nuclear holocaust and it was quite a little while before we were assured it was only an earthquake.

My first thought was of nuclear holocaust

In 1964 I was living on the end of the Spit in a house owned by the Abbotts and previously inhabited by my friend and sage Dick Haltiner, God rest his soul in peace. It was a nice little two room house with the outhouse attached to the side. Each month when the big tides covered the end of the Spit the accumulated smelly deposits were carried off to sea. I was located on the edge of the harbor and worked for Avery Sewell who had a little charter boat and skiff rental business. He was also the Harbor Master. To fill out my week, I worked part time at the Standard Oil plant where Mr. Crosby and John Waterman kept things in order for Chuck Abbott. Earl Hillstrand was running Land's End, the

Jack Estill

Edens were young men getting a fuel delivery business going and the Porpoise Room was under construction for Glen (G.G.) Sewell. Sunny Shelford and Royal Devaney were processing king crab. Max Devaney had a string of fishing boats. The Salty Dawg was a one room log cabin where a strange face in the winter was a cause for celebration. The only other cause being a day when the wind didn't blow on the end of the Spit. This was my second winter at the very end of the road and no Barefooters I knew of were speaking of cosmic bliss there. However, it was Heaven to a kid from southern California. Life was good.

Where was I in 1964 on the day of the great quake? I was on the end of the Spit sitting in the house tilted back in my chair with my feet on the table. I was enjoying a good book Dick Haltiner had given me for Christmas (Robert Service) and drinking a cup of hot Ovaltine when things started to shake. I think we had been having a few tremors before then and I didn't pay much attention until hot Ovaltine spilled in my lap and broke my concentration. Dumped on the floor and scrambling for the door, I nearly collided with a cylinder of freon which went bouncing by like a pogo stick. When I saw it jump out the front door I knew something extraordinary was going on.

Water was running out of the harbor like a great river. I made my way outside to see what was happening and when I stepped on the ground it was moving so much I couldn't stand. The ground was a spider web of cracks opening and closing and I was only able to stay upright by holding onto the front door. I looked down into the harbor and saw boats breaking loose and a few being sucked out of the harbor. Water was running out of the harbor like a great river. The boulders on the break water were jumping around like popcorn and then the whole breakwater went up the bay just as though it was being carried on a platter. It was covered by a big wave and seen no more.

I turned around to see a big crack open in the Spit and a little cabin, with a picturesque split rail fence in front and a little lawn, sink into the crack and rest at the bottom just like it was built there. I think it was destroyed by water a short time later.

One of my biggest worries was the Standard Oil tanks bursting and starting a fire. They were shaking around as though made of rubber. I remember being amazed steel could flex so much and not tear to pieces. The pilings in the harbor were flopping around like wet spaghetti also. When things stopped shaking it was real quiet and the water was still running out of the harbor like gang busters.

Avery Sewell came zooming up in his little red military Jeep and I said "Come on Avery, boats are getting away." And he said "#X@ those boats, let's get the hell off this Spit before the tidal wave hits." So I jumped in the Jeep and we raced down to the Porpoise Room where a half dozen men were working for G.G. Sewell and warned them to get to high ground. We then sped off the Spit and went to the Baycrest Motel and secured rooms for the night.

I was nervous about sleeping so close to that cliff with aftershocks so walked to town and toured the bars all night. I didn't drink much in those days but I can assure you most of the town was in the bars that night having a real good time swapping stories. Homer didn't fare too badly in the spirits department, but I ran into one guy who had come over by boat to get booze for Seldovia. He said the town was dry—and that was a disaster. All their bottles had broken.

Jack Estill

The next day I went back to my house on the Spit and it had a water line about half way up the windows. It was a mess. I didn't have anyplace else to stay so I set about raising it. I jacked it up and put 55-gallon barrels under it and on the next tide that night the water still came in, but not up to the bed. At first light I jacked the house up some more and put 12x12 beams on the barrels. I was above the water next tide and with a stove oil barrel attached to the side of the house things were homey again. I became a little nervous when I realized one night that the nearest land was miles away at high tide and thereafter kept my skiff tied to the door. My old 1946 GMC panel truck was covered with water at high tide and not much use.

One night shortly after the quake the wind made up out of the Southwest and breakers were crashing against the end of the house and water was squirting through the walls. Some runaway piling had lodged cross wise between the barrels and I thought each wave was going to topple me into the water. It was too rough to skiff in the dark for the base of the Spit and I thought how much better an earthquake on dry land was compared to the combers rolling across the Spit that night. But soon the tide went out as it will and the sun came up and all that good beach combing was waiting for me again.

I got some great pictures with my little Kodak camera while skiffing around on the day time tides. The Standard Oil tanks under water, Land's End awash and the end of the Spit miles out to sea. If I can find them I will send them along. Thirty years is long time to save something and I don't know if they survived. I feel lucky to have brought my carcass this far.

Judy White-Kruger
The Newspaper Kids

MARCH 27, 1964, WOULD BE A TIME that Alaskans would remember forever. It was a beautiful Good Friday in Homer. The sun was glistening off the clean, white snow as my brother, Roger, and I delivered newspapers. I was ten years old at the time. Rodger said "You wait here Jude, this old man is crazy." I plopped down in the snow to wait by the road as he took the paper to the door. I lay back and looked up at the clear, blue sky. It was so beautiful. A few white clouds floated up high and looked like fluffy cotton balls. Little did I know this was the calm before the storm.

I remember thinking how peaceful it was—at least until I heard a loud rumbling sound. The next thing I knew, the ground was shaking violently, and my brother ran from the old man's house screaming, "Let's get out of here." (He later told me he thought the old man was doing some sort of experiments.) I didn't know what to do because of the shaking ground. It seemed as though it would never stop, but finally, after four and a half minutes, it did. We both looked at each other in awe and quickly headed home. The huge front windows of the drug store were shattered. People were in a state of panic and rumors were spreading about a tidal wave.

We were surprised when we arrived home to find very little damage. The Pyrex coffee pot had flown off the stove top and smashed on the floor. The most amazing thing was that my mother's antique tea cups, that had been sitting on a corner shelf four inches wide, barely moved.

Homer, being a small town, had volunteer emergency services. My mother was the fire department dispatcher and my father the fire chief. When my brother and I reached the house, my mother was being bombarded with emergency telephone calls as my father stood by waiting for further information to act on. Dad then jumped into his truck and rushed to the fire station to join his crew. Mom also monitored the CB radio. There were a number of people living across the bay who might need assistance and Mom would be the one to get it for them.

Almost all of the telephone lines were out. The only calls getting through were emergency calls. Homer did not have any television then and the only methods of communication were radio, telephone, and newspapers.

Everyone hovered around the radio listening for more information. It seemed that Homer wasn't nearly as bad as Anchorage, Seward and Valdez. Huge fuel tanks had ruptured in Seward and Valdez and massive destruction covered the city of Anchorage. Homes in the Turnagain area slid off into the Inlet, never to be seen again. Roads throughout the state were ripped apart as though they were just lines on a piece of torn paper. People and cars were swallowed by huge crevices in the earth. Tall buildings were covered with numerous cracks.

The woman across the street from us would ... stand outside with her two children and would all scream together as loud as they could.

The fear of a tidal wave constantly remained in everyone's mind. Many people packed up their families and headed up the hill. As I sat there on the sofa waiting to see what would happen next, my parents argued over which one would take us up the hill. My mother thought dad should take us because she needed to remain with the emergency phones. My dad felt he needed to be there in case of fires or other emergencies. Needless to say, it is a good thing there was no tidal wave, because none of us left for the hill.

After the big quake, there continued to be many smaller aftershocks. The woman across the street from us would totally lose control with each tremor. She would stand outside with her two children and would all scream together as loud as they could. Once she stood under a tree and massive amounts of snow fell on her and the kids. My mother rushed over to help brush them off and to try to calm them.

The government sent aid of various types and Alaska slowly put herself back together. It is good to see how people join together and help each other in times of disaster. However, it is unfortunate that it takes a disaster to bring people together.

Aloma White
A Mother's Story

I T WAS LATE AFTERNOON ON MARCH 27, 1964. My two younger children were out delivering newspapers on their route. My daughter Sheryl came in, accompanied by her friend Mike, carrying a big bouquet of spring daffodils for me. I placed them in my favorite vase in the living room and thanked her.

My living room held an assortment of communication equipment used for various services; for Trans-Alaska Telephone I had the job of information operator, for the fire department there was the red telephone, or emergency hot line, and in the corner on my desk sat my CB radio that I used to contact the firemen. My husband, Frank White, was the local fire chief and somehow I had ended up with the job of answering the calls.

We were very proud of the CBs as we had built them ourselves after the fire department had voted against purchasing radios for the emergency vehicles. We had financed them personally and felt that they speeded up the emergency services a great deal.

I also monitored a channel on the CB and kept a schedule with several families across the bay as they had no phones.

The quake hit with a vengeance. The house moaned and groaned as the ground rolled beneath it. We had started an addition on the back of the house. It sounded like it was coming loose, snapping and popping. We all ran outside to see if any of the boards were actually coming off. Surprisingly they held, although some bowed.

Aloma White

Frank had been home at the time and he ran for his pickup, heading for the fire hall where he could be ready for incoming calls.

... the earth beneath my feet rose and fell and I ended up sprawled on the ground There was a little cabin across the road from our house where Shirley Ekron was staying in with her children. I looked toward her place in time to see her little ones running out of the house in their underwear. Shirley screamed and I tried to run to help her but the earth beneath my feet rose and fell and I ended up sprawled on the ground. Shirley's screams tore through the evening air as she flew out of the cabin trying to run toward me. My heart stood still as I scrambled to my feet calling out for her to hurry. She couldn't see the huge load of snow on the tree limbs that I was sure would fall on them at any minute. Somehow we all got into our house. I'm sure that it only took a few minutes but it seemed much longer. I got blankets to bundle the shivering children in and they curled up on my davenport.

Once they were settled I started what would end up being a five day vigil of calling people to see that they were all right, and being there for the incoming. One lady answered her phone in a shaky voice. I asked if there was any serious damage at her house. "Yes, I am soaking wet. I was sitting on the privy and the house was moving so badly that I couldn't get up. I had to sit there and be severely splashed." I had to smile. At that time we had no idea how wide spread the quake was.

My younger two children arrived out of breath and wide eyed babbling about the ground moving around. The house was a shambles. My unbreakable Corning Ware coffee pot lay in pieces on the floor. All of the books from the

shelf were laying in a mixture of water and crushed daffodils, scattered to the far corners of the kitchen.

A few feet from where the book shelves had set was a
knickknack shelf that held a few of my grandmother's delicate cups and saucers. It had not moved an inch.

In the next few days I stayed near the telephones and
radio taking the calls and reports. Frank was called to various places in his capacity as an electrician. The Spit was one
of the hot spots; attempting to keep electrical things dry as
it became more apparent with each rising tide how far the
Spit had sunk. Even traveling out to the Spit to do the work
was a problem as the tide deposited logs, kelp and etc. on
the road every twelve hours. Our pickup finally bit the dust
from too much salty wear and tear.

When we stopped by the drug store the next day we saw
the biggest mess ever as Howard Myhill and wife Beryl tried
to clear the floor of a combination of broken glass, sham-
poo, rubbing alcohol, perfume and etc. Even if the place
looked awful it sure smelled good.

Shirley Ekron returned to her home at Kasitsna Bay to
be with her husband in this upsetting time. I kept schedule
with them on the radio in the following days as the tides
got bigger. First the tide was near their porch, then splash-
ing at their door, then they were sitting down to eat dinner
in their hip boots and hoped that the water wouldn't float
the table.

People just cope.

John Child
As I Remember It

BEING FROM CALIFORNIA and experiencing many earthquakes, I knew what was happening when the trailer we were living in began to rock and roll without the music to go with it.

This wasn't like anything I had experienced before. It was like being in a skiff in a quiet harbor and all of a sudden a large boat passed by and made a big wake. But it lasted much longer than any previous quakes I'd experienced. I knew it was going to be destructive somewhere. I turned the radio on and there was nothing and the TV was dead, no power anywhere. I had the boat VHF radio in the front room, that was on the boat battery and that was our communications with the outside world. I switched it on the emergency band and listened. Warnings were going out to all the boats from the Coast Guard but nothing was getting to the crab fleet in Kamishak Bay across the inlet. Weather was keeping the fleet behind Mt. Augustine at anchor. I called the *Violet Ray* and told them what happened and gave them the Coast Guard warning.

It was cozy and comforting to be together with all our friends in an emergency situation.

I decided to get down to the harbor and check on the boat. I hopped into the jeep and started out the driveway only to be stopped by traffic coming in my driveway. Carol Deitz told me they were expecting a tidal wave and I best wait till the all clear signal was sounded.

We all gathered around the radio and listened, drank coffee while the ladies fixed food for the ten families we had suddenly acquired. It was cozy and comforting to be together with all our friends in an emergency situation. There were no reported injuries in our area. H.E.A. was on line shortly after the system could be checked. Looking back to when the quake first hit I can remember my daughter, Barbara, going out to a shed in front of the trailer to get a shirt. Looking through the front window I could see her standing in the doorway of the shed putting on her shirt. I told her to stay there till the wave action stopped because she might get her foot caught in the cracks. The ground was breaking up in frozen paddies and I was concerned about her. She put her hands over her head as if dancing a new step and hopped from paddy to paddy till she got to the back door. I had the door open and she jumped to the

Land's End   John Child

John Child

Standard Oil tank farm   John Child

threshold and into my arms.

She laughed it off saying "I knew what I was doing, Dad." My heart was still in my mouth so I didn't comment. That was my worst feeling and the boat was next.

The next morning everyone went home after a breakfast of sourdough pancakes, moose steak, eggs and coffee. I headed for the boat harbor with a friend to check on the boat and harbor damage.

The Spit had sunk seven or eight feet, but the road was still passable up to an eighteen foot tide. The Spit and harbor was our disaster. The rock that was built on sand fill was nowhere to be seen and there were only pilings sticking up where the floats were.

I could see my boat about 300 yards off the end of the Spit where the harbor was. We put the pram in the water and ran out to the *Mary G.* and looked her over. The

Mr. Beamer's Machine Shop   John Child

mooring cleat that the boat was tied to in the harbor was
still attached to the tie-up line. A 12 inch cleat with 2-5/8
inch bolts, nuts, and washers still attached. The surge had
pulled the bolts through the 8 inch thick mooring plank.
Some surge! The iron bark and part of the upper rail were
split and that was the extent of boat damage. I was lucky.

What a mess! The bay was cluttered with gas drums,
lumber, everything imaginable from around the buildings at
the end of the Spit and cabins around the bay.

Mr. Beamer had a machine shop that would be ruined
when the big tides came up in a few days so we gathered
Styrofoam from harbor floats and attached it under the
building and when the tide came in we towed it into the bay
and over to the dock to be picked up and put on high
ground. I can't remember where it went.

John Child

At the Standard Oil tank farm, the oil in the tanks had to be removed so they could make new bases for them. The Alaska Standard came in April to pump the oil out.

Soon after the bay was cleaned up and a moving company with portable jacks elevated Land's End above high tide.

Ralph Cowls, our first Mayor and the Corps of Engineers got together and made plans to clean up the Spit and get a new harbor started. I watched them drawing sketches in the sand. By 1966 the boat harbor was excavated and people were looking for installations of stalls and docking areas. The Porpoise Room, now relocated, overlooked it.

And it's been all politics from that day till now. I wouldn't live anywhere else in this world.

H. A. Thorn
An Editorial

HOMER AND THE ENTIRE STATE of Alaska have suffered a disaster the magnitude of which has seldom been known in the world.[†] We must all remember that in the first confusion many exaggerations and false rumors are bound to be spread. We're not discounting the terrible effects of the tragedy; however, let us stop for a moment and think of the possible good that can come from this.

From a doubtful working year we now have changed to the prospect of full employment for everyone.

We have lost our small boat harbor and the Spit seems to have a dubious future, but the small boat harbor had many faults which undoubtably [sic] will be corrected, and the first reports of the entire Spit sinking are greatly exaggerated. We feel confident that the United States government will give assistance and that the boat harbor and the Spit will be better than ever.

Homer can be thankful that our damage was light and that all our main facilities are still in good working order. From this disaster, the eyes of the entire Kenai Peninsula will be focused on Homer, for we will have to act as the central distribution point for supplies for the entire Kenai. We can not help but grow in stature and importance.

[†]H.A. Thorn was editor of the Homer News in 1964

H. A. Thorn

We are sure also that the south 48 will get solidly behind us; after all, if we can afford to pour money by the buckets full into foreign countries, we can certainly afford to take care of one of our own states. From a doubtful working year we now have changed to the prospect of full employment for everyone; we have to in order to rebuild.

So let us not despair but rather let us look to the future and work together to build a better Homer and a better Alaska.

Alaska Earthquake 1964
Where were you?

KODIAK

Heart of Kodiak with tsunami damage   U.S. Navy photo

Donald L. Darnell
The Destruction of Kodiak

O
N MARCH 10, 1964, I TURNED 16 YEARS OLD. I was living in Kodiak, Alaska, having moved there with my family in 1960 from Washington state. At that age I loved living in Kodiak. It was small and every one knew each other. It was a friendly place. It was one of those small places where everyone waved at each other as they passed cars, even though we would see each other every day. To me the island was a wild place and I loved that too. Within a short walk from town one could truly be out in the wilderness where there were plenty of bears, deer, and smaller critters. During the summer the town was a wild place as well. The town was wide open almost 24 hours a day and all kinds of wild people from villages around the island would flock to town for various reasons. Most of them would wind up whooping it up to their hearts content until their business was done and they would leave town. (Winter could be pretty wild, too, in Kodiak, but mostly I was kept indoors because of the weather.) Kodiak, after all, was one of those typical Alaskan towns that had a whole passel of saloons and bars, and just as many churches to match.

At the age of 16 I was totally involved with all the happenings of high school. I never was that good of a student, but I loved sports and all the social events that high school had to offer a 16 year old. Besides, I had just acquired my driver's license, so life was wonderful. My father worked as a civil service mechanic out on the Navy base, and my

Donald L. Darnell

mother worked in Kodiak's only department, store called Kodiak Commercial.

On the afternoon of March 27, 1964, my father had just returned home from work and my sister and I were home from school. Mom was still at work. Our house was a big old two story place about 2 blocks from downtown, up on a little knoll. There was a big gravel field out in front of the house, and a big old school house at the other end of the field. It was a typical March day, wet and blustery, cold but not freezing. I think the sound came just a little bit before the shaking started. At any rate, the sound was very loud, a very loud rumbling from inside the earth, much louder than all the sounds being made from everything shaking and falling. The shaking started small but rapidly got very strong.

None of us had ever been in an earthquake, but it only took us a second to figure what was happening. My dad hollered "Get out of the house!" and we made our way for the front door. It was hard to keep standing up and there were about 5 steps from the door down to the sidewalk. It was obviously impossible to walk down the steps, so we jumped one by one for the sidewalk which was rolling and moving from side to side. I remember that I missed the sidewalk and landed in the grass. It was a very short distance to jump, but I missed it because it moved.

The sound was incredibly loud. We made our way out of the yard and out into the gravel field because there were power lines swinging like crazy overhead close to the house. All of this, starting from when the shaking started, took about 15 seconds.

When we got out into the field there was nothing more to do but ride it out. To this day I remember the most overwhelming feeling being that I was totally helpless, and that there could never be a more helpless feeling than this. There was nothing I could hold on to and the most physically stable thing in my life was moving in all directions so radically that one could hardly stand up. The sound from the earth got louder and shaking got worse. I remember trying to talk to my father who was just next to me and we had to holler at each other.

There were all kinds of people trying to make their way out of their houses and get out into the field we were standing in. Some of them were crying and crossing themselves as they stumbled and tried to run.

To this day I remember the most overwhelming feeling being that I was totally helpless...

Some of the old women seemed to be chanting or perhaps saying hail-Marys.

We had a dog and he had managed to make it out of the yard and was beside us, but he had all four of his legs spread out wide and he was on his belly with his ears back. At that time I didn't know a dog could do that. He must have been crying but I couldn't hear him.

I could see windows shattering in several of the houses in my view, but I couldn't hear it, then I turned to look at the old school house at the other end of the field just in time to see a massive amount of windows shatter, and I couldn't hear that either. I could hear a few people screaming and crying hysterically but it was faint against the roaring rumble from beneath my feet.

The shaking seemed to go on for several minutes, but to this day I can't remember exactly how long the shaking lasted. All of my attention was focused on staying on my feet and watching everything around me move as though it were on a roller coaster ride. Buildings weren't falling around me, mainly because everything in Kodiak was made of wood, and I didn't see anybody getting killed, so actually it was quite exciting and thrilling.

As soon as the shaking started to subside, we all thought of Mom. Dad didn't quite know what to do. He didn't want to take us downtown to look for her and he didn't want to leave us alone, but before he could make a decision here she came kinda running up the road from town. She had been in the department store and a lot of the ceiling had fallen down but no one got hurt.

The family being back together, my thoughts and attention went to the ocean. I remembered the story of the earthquake in Hawaii and how all the water went way out and everyone went down to see it and then got killed by the tidal wave. I mentioned this to my dad so he put me on watch to keep an eye on the ocean while they surveyed the damage to the house. I could see the harbor plenty good from the front porch. Nothing seemed to be going on and I was starting to get bored when I realized that I couldn't see the break water any more. I rushed in to tell Dad and found them listening to a special announcement on the radio which was telling us to get to high ground.

What I found out later was that a series of small waves were coming in and out of town. Each one was a little higher and lower and faster. Our side of the island had sunk 8 feet so it didn't take much of a tide to cover the break water.

We hurriedly put a few things together and got into our car and headed for the road up Pillar Mountain. The town of Kodiak is built on the side of Pillar Mountain so we assumed we would get a good view of everything up there. Unfortunately, by the time anything started happening in town, it was too dark to see anything.

The Destruction of Kodiak

Kodiak Harbor after the tsunami   Daisy Lee Bitter

There was a real traffic jam. Literally everyone in town was trying to get up to Pillar Mountain except for those who were trying to save their boats or get them out of the harbor.

And then there were the famous Kodiak drunks who refused to leave the bars downtown even during the earthquake and even after the tides started washing through town. Finally it got dark, there was no electricity by this time, and the water was getting so high in town that they all decided to leave, but they had to form human chains, holding on to one another, to make it through the high water and debris.

By the time the real big waves were moving through town it was dark, and all we could do was hear our town being destroyed. In those days most people only had CB radios on their boats. There were a couple of cars near where

Donald L. Darnell

we parked that had CBs too and we could hear the fishermen talking to each other. It was a mixture of comedy and tragedy. Some of the more notable conversations were later printed in the first newspaper to come out after the wave. Some of the fishermen made it out to deep water and safety, but many were caught in the strong currents and swept in and out of town several times, crashing into and through the stores and houses that had been Kodiak. This is what we could hear. We could hear all the buildings and boats being smashed to pieces, and on the CBs we could hear the guys on the boats who didn't seem to have any control. Sometime during the night I fell to sleep and missed some of the most dramatic radio conversations.

Later that night, it must have been midnight or later, everyone figured it was safe to come down off the mountain. On the radio they were announcing that no one could go downtown, because there was some looting going on, and that emergency shelter was being set up at the high school. We went to the high school and got ourselves some cots to sleep on and some food, and then Dad and I decided we had to see if our house was still standing. We drove down as close as we could to town and found that the National Guard had set up road blocks and literally roped off the town. We parked the car a little way up the street, got out and crawled through the brush and grass and ditches for about 300 yards until we found our house still standing.

We got inside and got some sleeping bags and some more food and then made our way back to the car. My Mom was so glad to hear that the house was OK. I was glad too, but mostly all this was a big adventure to me and I knew there wouldn't be any school the next day. The next day they let us back into our house. It was a mess, with several things broken, but mostly it was OK.

The Destruction of Kodiak

I remember that the water pipes had frozen, and Dad had to crawl under the house with a torch to thaw them. He was under there when we had one of the many after shocks that were going on months to come. It scared him so bad he skinned up his knees real bad trying to get out then he remembered he had left the torch going under the house and he had to go back under there and turn it off.

That day was a day I'll never forget, it was almost too much to bear. My dad and I had obtained special passes to go downtown and help with emergency salvage. I walked the two blocks to where the town had been and it was gone. My heart sank and stomach felt terribly sick, and I sat down and cried. I cried a few times that day. Most of the stores and houses were gone. Those that remained were smashed beyond repair or gutted by water. There were other people wandering around in disbelief some of them were crying too, others just standing, shaking their heads, and others working like crazy trying to uncover something of value to them.

It was hard to figure out what had been where. Where buildings had been there were plenty of big boats and trash. My dad was helping to get an emergency road built through town and get an emergency generator working for power. It was total chaos. People didn't really know yet that the island had sunk 8 feet, and the fact that every high tide would just come right into town made matters even worse.

I spent the day trying to help a friend whose store had been swept out into the bay. We found it and he was interested in getting inside to see if the safe was still there with all his important papers. We got it to shore and when the tide went out we found that the floor had fallen out and there was no safe.

Donald L. Darnell

My family was lucky. Our house was nearly downtown but it was up on a little rise. The water went around both sides of us and left boats scattered everywhere. A big power scow came to rest about 150 yards off to one side of us. It had about 20,000 lb. of king crab in its holds which later became quite a problem.

A couple days after the quake we had a bad wind storm and because the breakwater didn't give protection anymore a lot more boats were washed up on the beach in town. As I walked through town I came upon what was left of the old movie theater and realized that my dad and I had been there the night before the quake and had seen the last movie ever shown there.

Amongst all the debris in town were thousands of whiskey bottles which came from all the destroyed saloons and liquor stores. I could see that a lot of the fishermen were taking advantage of their boats being out of the water and painting the bottoms.

Well, Kodiak is truly a unique place. Chaos was to rule for years to come, but in this chaos there were small bits of order, or should I say organization. Nobody knew what was going to happen to what was left of the town or harbor. It was clear that some decisions had to be made.

The saloon owners didn't wait for anyone. The very first places to spring up out of the mud and debris that had been Kodiak were several plywood shanty type saloons. Some you could only get to at lower tides, but that didn't seem to matter.

The next building to rise out of the mud was a makeshift food store. By this time it was common knowledge that the town was 8 feet lower than it had been.

Now here's the brilliant part. The powers at large decided that the town of Kodiak, the oldest settlement in

The Destruction of Kodiak

Alaska, built by Lord Baranof, who had been warned by local natives not to build it there and suffered earthquakes and
tidal waves at the same site before, should be built back at
the very same place that had just been destroyed. What they
did was to cover the entire town site with 8 feet of gravel fill
and build the town back where it had been before.

My life was drastically altered overnight. From the moment the earthquake struck it was never to be the same
again. The friendly little town was gone, and the attitude
and character of the place was gone too. What came next,
and for years to come, was an invasion of construction
workers and heavy machinery and what seemed like hundreds of dump trucks working day and night to cover up all
my memories of a place I had loved. They built back a ticky-
tacky mall type affair that had no character and left one
feeling cheap.

I suppose I suffer from "It ain't like it used to be." I will
admit to that. Compared to others I suffered and lost very
little. When I see on the news all the natural disasters that
affect so many people in our country, let alone the world, I
know how lucky I was, but still I can relate a little to one
who has lost his town.

Caroline Bacus-Venuti
A Tidal Wave Story

THE WEATHER WAS COLD AND CLEAR. It was perfect for ice skating. The ice on Kodiak's Island Lake was so thick that many people had parked their cars out on it. I was there with the church youth group from Idiak Baptist Mission for an ice skating party.

After skating for two hours, we gathered at the shelter on the far side of the lake for a potluck dinner. I remember that I had brought potato salad in one of my mother's large bowls. I was inside preparing the meal when I heard a loud noise and felt the building shaking. Thinking that boys were playing pranks up on the roof, I went out the door to tell them to knock it off.

What I saw upon opening the door was that the spruce trees were swaying back and forth, some of the tops even touching the ground. The ice on the lake was completely shattered, and all of the cars and trucks that were there shortly before had disappeared.

The ice on the lake was completely shattered, and all of the cars and trucks that were there shortly before had disappeared.

It was clearly apparent what had happened. All of the kids got together, in amazement at what we had observed. We agreed that we should get back to town to tell our parents about the "earthquake at the lake." (Oddly, we all thought that this was something that had occurred only there; no one realized at this time that it had happened statewide.)

Since we could no longer simply walk across the ice to the school bus that had brought us, we had to walk around the lake shore. This took a half hour to do, and I remember thinking that the shattered ice looked just as it would during breakup. There were great chunks scattered about the water's surface, and they continued to slosh back and forth in a disarrayed jumble.

We arrived back at the bus, got in, and the driver started back to town. As we approached the outskirts of Kodiak, we saw many people running about. They were loading things into their cars and trucks. Some were acting as if in a panic.

When we reached a bottleneck in the traffic, the driver stopped and asked a man what was going on. He was told that the radio had warned people there was a tidal wave coming and to get to higher ground.

The driver then turned to us and said that his responsibility was to get back to the mission, that in essence, we were now "on our own."

The bus emptied quickly, and I found myself feeling full of adrenaline, running the last mile or so home. I remember at one point wondering why I was still carrying the full bowl of potato salad, so I tossed it into the woods. For all I know, it may still be there in the bushes.

When I arrived at my home, Mom and Dad were quietly sitting in the living room. My sister was there, and the only one missing was my brother. He came in shortly after I did and told us what had happened downtown.

The dinner which had been on the dining table was all over the floor. There was no other sign of damage to the house, nor had I noticed any obvious damage to the neighborhood on the way home.

120

A Tidal Wave Story

We lived at that time on the shore of the channel which separates Kodiak from Near Island. There was nothing between us and the beach.

Even though we had been warned that there would be a tidal wave, we stayed and watched the water rise higher and higher in the channel until it was higher than I had ever seen on any tide.

Then it started to recede. As it did we could see many items afloat and going out to sea, including an unmanned fishing boat going backward and some small buildings. The water continued to empty seaward until the channel was dry. I remember having this strange urge to walk across to Near Island.

At this point my parents agreed that it was time to leave. Clearly the water would be coming back with some substantial force. We packed the car with some quickly gathered provisions. We had to beg Dad to bring the pets, and at one point I recall being in a teen-aged panic about my diary and my "jewels."

At last, all loaded up in our '59 Ford station wagon, we left and found ourselves in a long line of cars trying to get up Pillar Mountain. Most of the town was in this line. It was obvious that not all of us would get to the top.

It was a strange feeling sitting there trapped in this long line of traffic going nowhere. It was dark by now and the moon was full. Looking down at the town of Kodiak, all we could see was the reflections of the moon on the water which seemed to cover most of downtown. The electricity was off, so there was not the usual view of city lights.

We sat there and waited until someone came by and said there was a shelter set up at the high school. We pulled out and drove to the school where Civil Defense had set up facilities including handing out blankets and a soup line. We spent the night at the high school sleeping on the floor with other families.

In the morning we went home. Driving back to our house on Mission Road, we could see the results of the tidal wave—the town was a total wreck. Some roads were impassable because of debris. There were even boats far inland from the harbor.

When we reached our house, we could see where the sea water had reached about two feet deep inside. There was a layer of mud over everything, and the place smelled like very, very low tide.

Fortunately, we owned two homes. The other was shortly upslope from where we had lived. The water had not reached that high, so we simply moved in there.

The electricity was off and the furnace would not function. Dad cut a hole in the roof and installed a wood stove. We had an old water well that he uncovered so we had a source of fresh water. This was important as the town's reservoir had emptied when the dam collapsed.

One thing that comes to mind was that Dad worked on the reservoir shortly before the quake and had dropped a new hammer that we had given him into the water. After the quake we drove up there and he was able to walk over to that spot and find his hammer in the mud.

It took some time for things to get back to normal. A month of being without electricity or any of the other things that were considered normal. We were fortunate in that at that time most of us were not used to the modern convenience of supermarket shopping. This meant that there was much canned food put up. Mom cooked on the wood stove, and we had many people stop by to eat with us.

School was out for a month or so. The Navy established military control over essential services, establishing a curfew and patrols in the heavily damaged areas to prevent looting. The Civil Defense authorities put out a mimeographed daily news letter which told of availability of various services. This news was passed hand to hand as well as by mouth.

I recall that there were many fires set to burn throughout the town in order to eliminate hazards and to control rodents who became an immediate health problem.

For a long time after the quake, the beach combing along all shores was full of surprises. Things such as cases of food and many other goodies were found. One neighbor found enough rolls of fabric to last her a lifetime. She washed it all by hand.

Of all the things that come to mind when I try to remember that strange day back in 1964—the one thing that I consider most ironic was that had this earthquake happened twenty minutes earlier, all of the children that were out on that lake ice would have perished.

Norman Nault
The Year I Should Have Stayed in Bed

INETEEN SIXTY-FOUR WAS THE YEAR...
I probably should have just stayed in bed. To begin
with, my partner Pat and I had spent December of
'63 and the early part of '64 trapping on Aiaktalik Island off
the south end of Kodiak Island.

Things had gone very well. We had about five thousand
dollars worth of beautiful pelts packed in my twenty-four
foot double ended dory. We had all our gear plus a priceless
bidarka we had found and were taking it to give to the
Baranof Museum in Kodiak.

We were leaving Aiaktalik and headed over to Deadman's Bay when we got a bad surprise. Out of absolutely
nowhere a sneaker wave came at us in Alitak Bay and
swamped our boat. It was only twenty above zero. Before
we knew it we were on the bottom of the dory and had lost
everything we had to the sea. We were forced to kneel and
paddle for seven hours and, if it hadn't been for a real
miracle, our lives would never have been saved by the fishing boat *Decora* who rescued us.

The sneaker wave had been unnerving. I had never seen
anything like it. And even after the swamping incident I
thought the water was kind of "screwy" at times. If I had
known then the big earthquake was coming up, I think I
would have associated the two together some way.

Most of the people at Akhiok are Aleut. At that time Pat
and I re-outfitted ourselves by working at the cannery in
Lazy Bay on the south end of Kodiak Island. We went over
our outboard motors which had been underwater in the

swamping and got them to running. After that we went up the bay to Akhiok Village.

Akhiok probably had a population between seventy-five and one hundred. I had many good friends there. Fishing on their boats, working with them in the cannery, and playing with their kids made some of us pretty close. I guess I knew just about everyone by their first name. Akhiok always seemed like my home. Pat and I left our dory there. We had made a decision.

In a desperation move to get bankrolled again we were going to stand up to the bitter February weather and hunt some prime winter seal on Tugidak Island. (Tugidak is on the Trinity Island group off the south end of Kodiak.)

We knew things would be tough for us, but we never anticipated what was ahead. First of all we narrowly missed being killed in the plane that took us out to the island. No one knew it, but it had blown a tire on takeoff. If it had landed on the beach at Tugidak, as planned, and not on the water, like it did, I think we would have had it.

After Pat and I were on the island a few days, Tugidak got hit by one of the biggest storms it has had in this century. It was extremely cold and I estimated that in the middle of the storm the wind may have hit a hundred and twenty knots. Anyway, it rolled the grass up just like a carpet and tore up clam beds that had been on the island for ages and ages. How our little plyboard cabin held together, I'll never know, but I think we had a pretty close call.

If I had known the big earthquake was just about due, I would have probably tried to link that big storm with it some way, it was so unusual. But Mother Nature can do some pretty powerful things without punctuating them with an earthquake, so who knows? The sneaker wave and the storm could just have been a coincidence.

The Year I Should Have Stayed in Bed

Anyway, Pat and I got some good pelts off Tugidak. But the whole bottom fell out of our trip when the air service didn't send the right plane to pick us up. The one they sent was too small. We had to leave on that plane, so a good part of our pelts were left cached on the island. They were well packaged and would be fine, but we couldn't come back to get them until spring. We were sure upset.

We sent what fur we had into Kodiak for shipment into Anchorage and the fur buyer. Then Pat and I went to Fox Island not too far from the Lazy Bay cannery and Akhiok Village. We took on a big job that kind of fulfilled one of my dreams and built a nice log cabin on my setnet site there.

I worked very hard on the door of the cabin and even put a real porthole in it. The place really meant a lot to me and that's where we planned to live and fish when the season began. Things were going pretty good. When we needed money Pat and I would go in the dory over to the Lazy Bay cannery and work for a day or two.

On top of these trips it seemed like we always needed something at the Lazy Bay store. We'd go there in our dory and come back by way of Akhiok Village. Depending on how long we visited the village, we'd make a dash, usually in the dark, back to Fox Island where we had our beds. A friend of mine, the school teacher at Akhiok, Rod Newhouse, saw how inconvenient this was for us.

"Norm, you stay here at the school with me any time you want. That's a lot better than making a run over to Fox Island at night. Pat can stay here too, and we can visit." That's the invitation Rod offered and that's how the extra room at Akhiok School became "my room" when there weren't any other guests.

After the year I had been having, that room was just plain luxury to me. I had my own bathroom and lots of hot running water. Pat had a place to sleep downstairs, not like mine, but pretty fine. Even better than the cozy room, I really liked Rod, who was from Montana and a fine fellow. He enjoyed good conversation and company and we all became wonderful friends.

That's how it came to be that on March 26, 1964, after a day of hunting in the dory, Pat and I landed at Akhiok Village intending to stay a night or two.

I remember little Andy, eight years old, running down to meet us and begging to tie up our dory. He liked to do that and was always on the lookout for us. We sure enjoyed him.

We had dressed a reindeer out and stored it in the school freezer some days before. I planned on cooking a big reindeer dinner for Rod the next day, which was March 27.

I really don't recall too much about the next day except the water was so flat. Calm and still most of the day. I wandered around the village visiting with friends. I had called the air service in Kodiak some time before and they had assured me they were taking our hides out to the Kodiak air terminal right away for shipment to Anchorage. I was expecting a check in the mail any day.

That evening I cooked the reindeer meat in the school cafeteria. It was very clean and nice and cheery. I used the stove in the kitchen part and we ate on the table out in front of the counter.

Rod and Pat were there and Slim, one of my trapping buddies, had come down from Deadman's Bay. Everyone was in a good mood. The meat was delicious and we had fresh salad, which was a real treat. Someone said it was one of the best meals they'd ever eaten. That didn't hurt my feelings any. (No one guessed it might be our "last" meal.)

Just as we were finishing up, a very old man from the village (he looked close to ninety), stopped in for a visit. He couldn't see very well and he shuffled along slowly using a stick when he walked. He settled down in a chair next to the dining room wall and smiled his greetings all around. I was still sitting at the table and Rod had gone to the kitchen to do the dishes when it happened.

It started with a jolt. A terrible jolt! Then my chair was shaking wildly. The whole building was being violently warped back, forwards, and sideways, twisted every direction. There were loud noises. Wood snapped. Timbers groaned. Sudden fear gripped all of us.

The old man had been sitting across the room from me. He jumped up, forgetting all about his walking stick, and ran for the door with all the agility of a much younger person.

I made a leap for him. "Don't go outside!" I yelled. "The earth will swallow you!" By the time I reached him he had made it to the door and thrown it open. The light was good. The school yard where the kids played during the day was smooth and bare but rippling in large unfamiliar waves. It was hard to believe I was looking at earth.

I saw the ground open up. A huge crack like a big mouth yawned at me then snapped closed. I saw this happen again. I grabbed the old man and shoved him back. Somehow I got hold of a chair and sat him down in a doorway inside the school.

Then I reeled toward the kitchen. There was Rod, still standing by the sink. He was swaying back and forth. In his hands were a plate and a towel. He just stood there drying the plate. Around and around went the towel. Rod saw me. Faster and faster went the towel over the plate. I saw the fear in his eyes and a kind of hypnotized look on his face.

"Do you always wipe dishes in an earthquake?" I barked.

"Sometimes," he rasped.

Everything in the storeroom had begun to fall. Big gallon glass jars of mustard, peanut butter, pickled beets, olives and countless other things slid off the shelves and were smashing down on the cement floor. The crashing noises were alarming and frightening. It was too dangerous in the storeroom to go in.

I was no stranger to earthquakes. When I was a prisoner of war in Japan, I had managed to live through twelve or thirteen devastating ones. Somehow that seemed to be giving me an extra understanding of what was happening now.

Once a building in Japan, our sleeping quarters, had collapsed around my buddies and me. The timbers crashed down and the walls fell away. Some were injured, but I had been lucky.

Now, the shaking didn't seem to want to stop. I lurched back to the door and opened it. The school was set on pilings and had been built on a rock. It was a little higher than the rest of the village and was almost brand new. My mind was telling me it was new, sturdy and maybe the best place to be.

But standing in the door and trying to keep my balance was changing my mind. The whole building was swaying. It looked to me like four or five of more feet in each direction. (No! Maybe eight feet! Things seemed so out of perspective.) "This thing is going to fall off these pilings!" I told myself in shock.

I yelled back at Rod to turn off the stove and the gas and everything else. I think he was way ahead of me and already somewhere doing that. A fire was a disaster we didn't need. The earth was still rocking.

The Year I Should Have Stayed in Bed

Then I saw Klumpy, the village chief, half staggering and half running toward me. I don't know how he made it. When he saw me in the doorway he yelled, "Run for your life! Big water coming!" The school swayed and Klumpy came to a stop.

Behind Klumpy I could see frightened people running crazily for high ground. Most of them didn't seem to be taking anything with them. I thought of little Andy. It was fifteen or twenty above zero. Very cold. The school might be a good place for them. But again, it might fall down any minute. And big water! A tidal wave!

I'd been in one of them in 1941. A three foot wave on Wake Island. It had been frightening because there was no high ground to run to. I shouted at Klumpy to make the people take blankets and tarps. Tents and matches, too. There was probably time to get those things.

Klumpy nodded at me like he agreed. "You come," he motioned toward the running people. "Listen," I yelled, "I'm going to try and stay here and cook for you. Up the hill.... You're going to need food."

"You drowned," he muttered. Klumpy turned and ran off. Someone came and fetched the old man with the walking stick and helped him up the hill. The building pitched and shook. "Just be sure you send someone down the mountain to help pack the food!" I shouted at his back with a shaky voice, but loud enough so I knew he heard.

I wasn't particularly confident with my decision to stay in the school. As a matter of fact, I was pretty scared. But, after all, I had been in earthquakes before and a tidal wave too. But it's true, I thought. This school might fall down! I don't think I'll drown. I'm too high. Sixty feet.

The deciding factor for my staying, though, had been memories. Memories of freezing cold nights in prison camp without blankets, without shoes and without food. These were especially vivid as I watched mothers with babies, old grandmothers, old men, struggling to get up the hill.

These were my friends. Everyone was helping everybody else. I was glad to see younger people running, bringing blankets and clothing, taking older folks by the arm, even carrying some of the older children. Twenty above zero is cold weather, even for hardy people..., I would stay and cook.

The earth did the hula dance. I'm sure a lot of us were thinking that this really might be the end of the world. Maybe the shaking would never stop. Every once in a while I could hear the words, "Big water coming!" float up to me.

"Aren't you going?" Rod yelled as he left.

"Think I'll stay and try to cook for everyone," I hollered as he ran by. Pat came up and said he was staying. I don't remember what Slim did.

In reality, after about the first eight minutes, the worst shaking had stopped. But strong aftershocks came continuously to rattle our nerves.

Now the village was deserted and Pat and I waited alone in the school for the tidal wave to hit. The marine radio blared in our ears. Right after the earthquake hit the radio had broadcast the tidal wave warning. The warning told us we probably had an hour before the wave was predicted to arrive. At that point I wasn't taking too much stock in predictions. I felt like something could happen at any minute.

Mostly, I just rode out the aftershocks as I stood and looked out the door, my eyes riveted to the water in the bay. As I remember, the tide was low. Once in awhile I'd let my gaze wander to the village below me. There wasn't a sign of life. I felt confident that everyone had made it up the hill.

The Year I Should Have Stayed in Bed

I can't begin to tell you the shock I got when I saw the wave. A wall of water forty or fifty feet high was suddenly in the bay and racing toward the village. It's hard to describe here just how fast it was coming. Its speed and height horrified me. This was a wall of ferocious, foaming, "monster" water and it seemed to be traveling at jet speed. How fast? All I can say is I saw it. Then it hit. That fast.

Sixty feet above the village was not enough. Now I knew I might die. The wave made a terrible roaring noise. I thought the school would shake apart as the giant wall of water slammed into the beach with insane thundering momentum and blasted into the houses. I think the ground shook harder than it did during the earthquake.

There was a horrible groaning and screeching and wailing below me as glass broke, timbers split and metal bent and gave way. Some of the houses, sheds, shacks, and boats were just lifted up and smashed together until they splintered like kindling.

I stood stunned in the doorway of the school. I saw a small amount of water flooding underneath me around the pilings that held the building up. Fear had overwhelmed me for a while but now I began to sense a change. The water was quieting down. It was like the wave had paused to take a breath. Then I heard a great sucking type sound as the water began to race back toward the ocean taking masses of debris and rubble with it. I guess I was shaking.

Now what I was seeing was almost beyond what I can describe. First I had seen the bay with the tide out and the quiet deserted village beneath me. Then the wave had come.

Norman Nault

Now, just a few minutes later, I was watching a bay full of *everything!* Everything that would float was washing out into the bay. I have never seen so many fifty gallon drums in my life. The water was jam packed with stuff. Lots of lumber, parts of sheds and houses, bottles, cans, dog houses, you name it. Everything was dipping and bobbing away together.

I stood and watched for some time. I could hear the muffled voices coming over the radio inside the school. I wondered what they were saying and I also knew there was lots of work to be done, so finally I turned and went in.

While we listened to the radio, Pat and I started to clean up the kitchen and salvage all the usable food. I got the stove turned on and started a huge stew with the reindeer. It was a shake, rattle and roll affair in the school. Both Pat and I were jumpy as hell.

We didn't know what to expect from the water. We didn't have much defense if it hit hard in the dark. On the radio we heard a boat at the near-by village of Kagoyak. Some of the village men had gone up to the lake above the village to get their skiffs. While they were up there the dam had broken above them. Some had drowned.

Pat and I knew how the little houses were nestled around the lagoon there at Kagoyak. The situation seemed very frightening and it was hard to tell on the radio just what was happening. The water came in again. Not as high as the first time but what we could see of it in the dark was scary enough. It never came with the terrible force of the first wave either. But it was sure raising havoc with everyone who was in a boat and lots of others as well.

We were listening to people on the radio who needed help. There was nothing we could do. Boats from the lagoon by Kagoyak were calling. One boat was trying to get into the lagoon. The boat would just get started and then report that all the water was out of the bay and they were stuck on the bottom. Then they would come on the radio again and say they had water and were coming into the lagoon. Then they would go dry again. Everyone was really scared. As I remember, where we were, the tide went in and out about nine times during a very short period.

But we survived the night and in the morning Pat and I got the food ready. I guess I wasn't surprised when nobody came down the hill to get it. I knew they were too frightened and I didn't blame them.

We sure had a struggle getting that food up to them by ourselves in that frigid weather. It was about two days before anyone would come down. The sad part for all of us was that one little baby died on the mountain. I'm not sure what the causes were.

In spite of the devastation caused by the force of the wave and water, there were quite a few houses left standing. A lot depended on how far they were above the beach. Many of them had been flooded or badly damaged and weren't fit to live in.

When the people came down the school was the center for everything. I stayed there and cooked for them a few days and did what I could. The Red Cross arrived and a lot of carpenters from Canada. A load of lumber came, donated from some states in the lower forty-eight. The people who got there to help were great and everyone in the village was so thankful. In bad times good people always pull together.

The people in Ahkiok suffered a great loss, but were more fortunate than the people in the village of Kagoyak. People had died. And most of the village buildings were not usable. The devastation was so bad, it never was built back.

As for me, I had lost everything again. My cabin and outfit on Fox Island were washed away. My furs, awaiting shipment in Kodiak had been lost when the warehouse had been destroyed by the wave in Kodiak. The stash of salted hides I had left on Tugidak were gone. My dory had disappeared and now I was low on cash. But I had my life and my health and God was watching over me. I knew I could start over, and that is what I set about to do.

©1994 Norman Nault

Jan Bunker Needham, 1994
for Robert Earl Needham
Tsunami

I HOPE MY MEMORY SERVES ME WELL.[†] It would be better if Bob Needham himself were telling you this, but he died in a plane crash in 1982 over by Dillingham on his way from Anchorage to Togiak in his own small plane. He told me about the big earthquake in Alaska before he met and married me in 1968.

In 1964, Bob was a teacher in the village of Afognak on Afognak Island near Kodiak. He had a fishing boat that he chased salmon with during the summers, and he kept it anchored offshore in front of the village, which was situated in a curving bay at the base of a mountain.

The school was government-built on a knoll at one end of the village. A sturdy frame building with a basement where the heating system and supplies were located. Schools were usually designed as autonomous units in villages that often did not have many amenities.

The night of the big quake, Bob said the village was having a town meeting in the church in the center of the village. He hadn't attended and was up at the school listening to the radio chatter about damage around the state. The village had withstood the shake without much damage and he wanted to hear the news of other

...when he stepped out of the school he could hear the gravel rolling on the beach...

[†] Written by Jan Bunker Needham for Robert Earl Needham.

areas. It was the tsunami warnings that were chilling. He thought he'd better get down to the village meeting—when he stepped out of the school he could hear the gravel rolling on the beach, so he ran to the meeting. He went inside and told a couple of the elders to come outside. When they heard the rocks rolling down the shore as the water was being sucked back off the beach, they reacted immediately. The villagers were told to evacuate as fast as they could, head up the mountain side, don't wait around, get out, now. The tsunami hit the village and totally wiped it out, but the people were safe on the mountain side. Bob had gone back to the school knoll at the side of the bay instead of up the mountain. The basement had windows so Bob had used towels, rags, etc., anything he could find, closing the windows and packing them against leaks. The water had risen right up around the windows but not come in. The school knoll was out of the main force angle of the tsunami and had been spared.

The next day Bob saw that most of the boats in the bay had been washed up and smashed or sunk, except his. He said he'd always anchored his with a very long scope on his anchor line — his boat had risen up with the waves and back down again, it was OK. With a dry basement, Bob had the main food and heat left in the village. He and his family fed and sheltered a lot of people in the school during the next few days until help could get to them.

The radio reports of the damage continued for days. But Bob said he'd felt about the worst when listening to a boat that first night, called the *Spruce Cape*, which had washed over the breakwater out of Kodiak Harbor on the first wave and was trying to get around the island out of the projected wave path, fearing the next wave surges. The captain gave his position over the radio just as the next wave hit him—he was off Spruce Cape—there were no survivors.

Bob was later to fly around the countryside with members of a team from the Lions International Service Organization, who had volunteered to help the Afognak Village residents relocate in a safer site. It always perplexed him that the village elders insisted on calling the new village Port Lyons instead of Port Lions, after all the help they had received.

©1994 Jan Bunker Needham

Alaska Earthquake 1964
Where were you?

CENTRAL PENINSULA

Laura Hendricks
Isn't It Awful ... ?

IT WAS A LOVELY SPRING DAY in the Morro Bay Cayucos area of California. We were on our way back home to Alaska, and had stopped in California to visit good friends, Brownie and Kaye. Their pleasant home overlooked the Pacific surf and oil docks below.

We planned to spend a night with them, renewing old memories. Then we'd be on our way North. We always enjoyed driving the Alaska Highway in March. We looked forward to the long, white miles that we'd be traveling soon.

There was so much to talk about, Kaye turned off the radio. No one even turned on television that night! We went to bed without listening to the evening news on March 27, 1964.

In the morning, golden and bright with flowers, Reg and I drove our old Aero-Willys to town for a few supplies before heading North. We saw a man half sprawled on one of the sidewalk benches and to our surprise we recognized him as another Morro Bay friend. We were not too surprised to see Bert, but he was weeping uncontrollably! Between sobs he wiped his eyes and leathery cheeks with a wrinkled bandanna.

"Bert," I said, as I rushed over to him, "What's the matter?"

When Bert saw us, he actually looked as though he had seen a ghost. There was a sudden look of disbelief, amazement and joy radiating from his face.

"Oh, Reggie, Laura, you're not dead! You're here! Isn't it awful what happened to Alaska?"

Laura Hendricks

There's been a killer earthquake and everyone's dead. Alaska's gone!

"What do you mean," I gasped! "Awful? Alaska? What happened!"

"Oh, it's gone. There's been a killer earthquake and everyone's dead. Alaska's gone!"

Stunned, we grabbed the morning paper and for the first time saw the frightening headlines. After reassuring Bert that we were safe, we left him and rushed back to Brownie and Kaye's. At last we listened to the radio and heard the latest news; a magnitude 8.6 earthquake had bludgeoned our part of Alaska!

As we dashed around getting our gear finalized for Alaska, we anxiously listened to each emergency broadcast. We didn't know for sure what was happening to people in our home state. Alaska was cut off from the world except for the information short wave operators were able to send. Working hour after hour, they relayed news and helped families find each other.

As a result of the quake, a killer tsunami wave struck Crescent City, California. People drowned along the northern beaches! We suddenly remembered the sound of anchor chains rattling out in Morro Bay last night.

"Strange," Brownie had said, "I've never heard those oil tanker chains before. I wonder what's up?"

Now we realized the ships had pulled their anchors and headed for open seas hoping to escape the huge waves that were expected even as far south as Cayucos.

We had enjoyed that evening with our friends. It was full of talk and laughter and shared memories. Providentially, we didn't know that, as we chatted on, our world was being shaken unmercifully.

We were in a state of shock and anxiety. The fragmented news we were able to gather increased our fears. We placed a fast phone call to Anchorage friends, Glennister and Steve. Amazingly, we got through at once! Yes, things were terrible! Yes, they personally were OK. Many homes were gone. Theirs was damaged but livable. Downtown Anchorage was cordoned off. Yes, it was still winter in Alaska. Come at once, they had room for us.

So we drove our Willys north. Now we were actually traveling those frozen white roads we anticipated. But what a difference in our expectations!

Naturally, we were concerned about all of Alaska, especially Anchorage, the population center of the state. However, our special memory and worry was our little brown cabin at Clam Gulch. Those memories haunted us as we pushed on through the winter passes. Our cabin was a historic one, perched right on the bluff above Cook Inlet. Feeding our anxiety was word that the bluffs had failed in Anchorage, tumbling scores of homes into the Inlet. Would that be the fate of our Clam Gulch cabin?

When we finally got to Anchorage, weary from the intensity of our drive, we were shocked to see the condition of 4th Avenue and the rest of downtown. In the past, we had lived on L Street right on the edge of the bluff. Now that apartment was 11 feet west of where it had been when we left!

There were many changes, some subtle and others glaring. Everyone had a frightening story of what happened to them when the earthquake struck on that gloomy, overcast Good Friday.

For some reason, which I've forgotten, we had a VW van filled with winter clothes, food and supplies. Anxious to get to Clam Gulch we planned to leave the faithful Willys in

Laura Hendricks

Anchorage and drive the van around Turnagain Arm and on to the Kenai Peninsula.

However, after several tidal changes, it became obvious that the whole land mass had sunk. It was clear to us that until bridges were rebuilt and roads raised, no one could drive around Turnagain Arm. The notorious tides were wildly unpredictable now. Most of the bridges had collapsed. How would we overcome the obstacles and get our van down on the Peninsula and to Clam Gulch?

Our anxiety level was so high that when an enterprising cargo company put a C-130 plane in service, we made an instant decision to load the van on the plane and fly toward our home.

They landed us south of the Kenai River. There, we heard that the Kasilof bridge, further south, had withstood the shocks and was probably safe to drive. So we continued on, not knowing from mile to mile what we'd find.

There seemed to be an eerie silence as we drove the familiar landscape. The road was roller coaster but navigable. The Kasilof bridge appeared to be safe, so, apprehensively, we crossed it and drove on to Clam Gulch. We were especially worried about our cabin since it was so close to the edge of the 300 foot bluff.

Our boat, the *Alaska Lass*, was on a trailer beside the cabin. There was no apparent damage but we could see tracks in the snow where the boat had been thrust forward and backward with the power of the quake!

We had placed a spare front door key on a nail driven into a spruce six feet above the ground. For some reason it seemed to be missing! Fortunately, we had a key with us and we apprehensively opened the cabin door.

To our amazement, our limber, Russian-built cabin was undamaged! The only item out of place was a Mexican vase

146

which had tumbled to the middle of the floor where it stood upright and unbroken!

Later as we talked to our neighbors, we found that during the quake, trees had actually touched the ground from side to side, as they whipped and threshed around. Our spruce had become a giant sling shot and hurled our key far into snow covered tundra. We never saw the key again.

We didn't understand why our losses were so small compared to others. Seward, we heard from those who had fled that port city, had suffered terribly. Within a few days we drove that way to see if we could get through the damaged roads and roller coaster bridges.

We must let others who experienced the quake describe Seward's destruction. For though we were terrified by after-shocks and slept with our important papers and emergency winter gear beside the bed, we hadn't actually been here while the great shaking was going on. No, we had been in beautiful Morro Bay, laughing and reminiscing with Brownie and Kaye. Now we were headed for Seward, Alaska where the worst had happened.

Our understanding of the horror and fear felt by those who had been in Alaska during the quaking was heightened when we talked to hitchhikers along the mangled way. They had survived the wave and the fire, but had lost everything.

... all persons we talked to said they had thought the world was coming to an end as the convulsions went on and on.

None of these haggard refugees made light of their experiences. Without exception, all persons we talked to said they had thought the world was coming to an end as the convulsions went on and on. There was no humor expressed, just thankfulness.

Laura Hendricks

No, there was no levity about what was probably the most violent earthquake to ever hit the North American continent. We, as bystanders and latecomers, joined our friends and neighbors in prayers of thankfulness that all of us had escaped the violent earthquake of March 27, 1964.

Debbie Poore
One Day in March

I GREW UP IN KENAI, the eldest daughter of Kenai River homesteaders. And I watched my father cry when word came that Grampa Poore was dead.

Good Friday, evening
Listening to news on TV at our baby-sitter's.
HARD-fast! Earthquake!!

John Kodysz yelled to us to get out, he didn't know if the large one-room log cabin would hold. Glass dishes, figurines **Frozen spruce trees whipped from side to side...** and pictures careened out of cupboards and crashed all around us as we struggled desperately to crawl across the floor. Two adults and eight children tumbled along the plywood floor and out the door to sit and sway on the porch and perched on hoods of cars that rolled first two feet forward then two feet backward. At least sitting on cars we felt we wouldn't be swallowed by the ground cracks we expected. Cold War training at school had this ten year old convinced that it was the end of the world. The earth was falling apart.

Frozen spruce trees whipped from side to side, somehow bending to touch the ground with each undulation.

Mom, driving down the driveway, thought we were sick and yelled to us hysterically asking what was wrong before she felt the ground shaking uncontrollably.

It seemed to last forever and ever.

149

Debbie Poore

Eventually we went home to check on everything. The fuel tank had fallen off the tree so we had no heat in our house. Dishes and food had fallen out of the cupboards and broken into a mess on the floor. The TV had fallen forward off a chest of drawers and landed in a dirty-clothes basket. Mom and Lisa and I went back to Kodysz's to spend the night in their company tucked into sleeping bags on the floor. The adults stayed up through the night riding out the aftershocks and listening to emergency bulletins on the radio.

Dad and four year old Tracy had gone to Minnesota to Gramps's funeral and upon landing back in Seattle heard that a tremendous earthquake had destroyed the Kenai Peninsula. They flew into Anchorage less than 24 hours after the quake and must have marveled at the unending damage. They managed to charter a small plane to Kenai and then caught a ride out to the homestead. I can still remember how very good it was when they arrived home, safely. Having our family back together was a comforting blessing.

Dad managed to find an unending crack across the frozen marshlands—the tangled, matted mosses had been cleanly severed and separated 4 inches, and he could stick a rod down and not touch bottom.

Our town did not suffer as much as many others. Yet food and other supplies had to be flown into Kenai because only one bridge on the Sterling and Seward Highways had withstood the earthquake, the curved one over Canyon Creek.

One Day in March

Even now, it's the second wave of an earthquake that captures my undivided attention and triggers an adrenaline rush—that remembered feeling that the shaking isn't going to stop, ever.

Poopdeck Platt
My Big Easy Chair

I REALLY DON'T HAVE ANYTHING INTERESTING to tell you about the earthquake. I was winterman at the Columbia Ward's Cannery at Kenai at the time and I happened to be sitting down in my big easy chair in the living room when it started. My wife had just come to the archway between there and the kitchen when it started. She was trying to hang on to the wall.

I hollered, "Sit down!" and she had to crawl to get over to the couch; after a half hour (4½ minutes by the book) it stopped. I made a dive for the stove and shut the oil off as I was sure the brick chimney would be cracked, if not down. It wasn't. It was one of the two chimneys out of eleven at the plant that weren't damaged. I took a quick look around then.

Bernice and I jumped in the car and ran ten miles down to where my daughter and her family lived to see how they made out but they were out checking on their neighbors, so we didn't find them. On the way home Bob Schmid flagged us down and said watch out for a tidal wave. I said, "Too late, it's already gone by." As it happened, the quake came at low tide and the wave was headed away from Cook Inlet toward Kodiak where it did a lot of damage.

One peculiar thing; the upper Inlet had sunk so much the tide had to run up inlet for 24 hours instead of changing at 12 as normal. One other weird thing; we had had a lot of cold weather before it snowed so the ground was frozen down about six feet. Well, looking across the Kenai duck flats there were black streaks in weird patterns where the

Poopdeck Platt

ground had cracked and snapped open and shut enough to
squirt mud in the air.

154

Roy E. Hoyt Jr.
Among the Missing

SINCE IT IS NEARING THE THIRTIETH ANNIVERSARY of the "Great Alaskan Shake" and after looking over the names of retirees in *Our Time* it brought to mind the time I was among the missing.

The Hoyt family had moved from Cape Yakataga to Kenai on March 17, 1964. I had purchased an automobile in Anchorage and flew up there on my day off March 26th to pick it up and drive it back to Kenai. I stayed with Jim and Bernice Formella that night.

When I realized that the automobile paperwork and insurance would not be completed until in the early afternoon I called Jack Hummel, the FAA Chief, and was granted a day of annual leave for the 27th.

I departed Anchorage around 14:30 hours and stopped at the Portage House on Turnagain Arm for a rest and refreshment stop as it was snowing rather hard. I considered spending the night there but decided I could make it through the hills before dark and proceeded toward Kenai. It was a good thing I made that decision.

As I passed Millie Eaton's Kenai Lake Lodge the car began to sway on the icy road and the trees were bending across the road. I thought, "one hell **... a little crevasse over a foot wide was swaying back and forth ...** of a wind here." As I was rounding the curve on the approach to the Kenai Lake bridge the bridge jumped about thirty feet in the air and fell into the water. I put the car in HIGH WHOA, dismounted, and about ten feet in front of me was crevasse a little over a foot wide that was swaying back and forth. I got out of there in a hurry and parked across from the lodge just off the highway on the lake side. I watched the ice on Kenai Lake break up, turn over in the lake, and the lake flow toward Seward. All the while I had an 8mm movie camera and a 35mm camera sitting on the scat beside me and I didn't take a single picture.

I spent the night at the lodge as you could not get past Summit Lake to the north, Moose Pass to the east, or Kenai Lake to the west.

About 11:30 the morning of the 28th a Cessna 180 piloted by Loren Horn of the Kenai FAA spotted me in front of the lodge and landed at the Quartz Creek strip behind the Sunrise Inn. Loren told me that I was among the FAA missing in the earthquake and that he was looking over the highway from Kenai to Anchorage for me. They knew that Cal Ward and Miles Pierson had seen me at about 13:30 on 5th Avenue the afternoon of the 27th, across from the new J.C. Penney store, and no one had seen me since.

Along with myself, Horn loaded the Kenai Magistrate, Jess Nickolas, weight well in excess of 300 pounds, his wife, Carolyn, and their new baby into the airplane. One hell of a load for a C180 on a short strip. By all of us leaning as far forward as we could we became airborne and I reported to the FAA for my 16:00-24:00 watch.

Two weeks later, after a Bailey bridge was installed across the Kenai Lake mouth, Jack Hummel drove me to the lake to retrieve my car from Millie.

The Kenai FAA complement at that time consisted of: Larry Lawton, Station Manager; Pete James, Foreman Mechanic; Loren Horn, Mechanic; Frank Hall, SET; Dean Smith, ET Trainee; Jack Hummel, Facility Chief; ATCS'es

Ken Jordan, Walter Hart, Tom O'Malia, Jack Leonard, Julian "Jit" Spillers and myself.

To this day, every time I cross the Kenai Lake bridge the episode returns to my mind and I wonder what would have happened had I decided to stay overnight at the Portage House.

Alaska Earthquake 1964
Where were you?

VALDEZ

Barbara Tyndall
Have Mercy On Us!

IT BEGAN SUDDENLY. THERE WAS NO WARNING. One moment it was peaceful and still. The next moment the ceiling and walls were lunging. There was tremendous noise, terrible rumblings from the earth's belly. My first instinct was to get out of the house and out from under the careening ceiling.

"It's an earthquake!" I shouted. "Somebody get Johnny!" I flew past my brothers and out the back door.

The house was moving so far it was covering Mom ...

Just moments before my mother had been putting dinner on the table. I had just stood up in the living room to come to the table.

Mom grabbed my one-year-old brother, Johnny, highchair and all, and stumbled onto the back porch. She wasn't there long. The force of the quake knocked her off the porch and next to the foundation of the house. The house was moving so far it was covering Mom, the baby and highchair with every pulse. Somehow, my thirteen-year-old brother Pat managed to get Johnny out of the chair and pulled them both up to where I was perched on a three foot snow bank. There we sat and rode out the 1964 earthquake in Valdez.

Dishes were breaking in the kitchen, the house was creaking and groaning, the ground rumbled and growled. The snow was breaking up all around us like a giant jigsaw puzzle But the eeriest of all was the swish, swish of the trees around our house as they bent back and forth, touching the ground on either side. Some were six to ten inches in diameter but they swayed like willow branches and kept us from moving past them. Power lines were flailing overhead. "Have mercy on us! Have mercy on us!" My mother's words sent chills through my heart. I thought I was going to die.

It went on and on. The ground moved under us like the waves of the sea. We pitched and rolled and clung to one another on our little island of broken snow. Cars were rolling up and down the streets. There was no place to run to, no solid ground. There was a slight lull before it became more violent, threatening to knock us off our tiny spot.

Finally, with a crash, it stopped. A long mournful wail from a ship's horn called from the harbor. As if on cue, water gushed up from cracks in the streets, doors flew open and people rushed out of their homes and congregated in the street.

I was barefooted and the ground was frozen but I was afraid to go back into the house. Sven, the baker, and his wife Eleanora, joined us in the street. They were in their pajamas. Sven got up so early for work at the bakery that they had just gone to bed for the night when the quake hit. We all climbed into their car to get warm. A man pulled up and told us the entire dock and cannery had disappeared into the sea.

People were saying we would have a tidal wave. A neighbor across the street told us Valdez couldn't get a tidal wave because of the narrows. As it turned out she was correct However, we were taking no chances. We ended up stranded in backed up traffic along the tide flats. If a wave had come, we would all have been swept away.

Eventually, my dad found us and took us home. He had been driving into Valdez from Tok at the time of the quake.

He had seen water spouts hundreds of feet high coming out of the river as the ice cracked. The closer he got to town, the worse things looked. When he came to the first bridge there was a line of traffic waiting on the opposite side. He crossed over and asked them what was going on. The man told him they were wondering if the bridge was safe to cross. Dad had just proven it was. They got into their cars and drove off.

Back in town we went to Sven and Eleanora's house because they still had lights and heat. We did not. It was dark by now. Mom put my brother Johnny to bed in a back room. I didn't like for us to be separated. I was so thankful we were all alive but very untrusting of the ground under my feet. The ground felt like Jello. Every time a truck or car passed, the house shook.

Someone turned on a radio. "Valdez is wiped out. Valdez is wiped out," it announced. We blinked at each other and laughed nervously.

About 11:00 pm someone said, "They'll give us a signal of three if we are supposed to leave town." Just then the lights went out. They came back on. They went out again. They came back on. The third time they went out we all jumped up and ran outside. The sky was on fire. The oil tanks were burning. A fire whistle wailed through the night. All the men rushed toward the blaze. I hated having my dad leave but they were back shortly. Burning oil was floating into town on top of the tide and there was nothing to fight it with. A police care circled the town. Its loudspeaker blared, "Evacuate the town. Evacuate the town."

We left Valdez with Sven and Eleanora. We parked for awhile along the flats where many were already out of their cars watching the fires. It was there we began to learn of those who had died on the docks. One was a boy in my-

Barbara Tyndall

freshman class, another a boy in my brother's class. A family of five and the coach and his two preschool boys all disappeared on the docks. Only one body was ever found.

As we drove through the night, the snow was ghostly on Thompson Pass and the full moon had literally turned blood red. It was Good Friday and many of us thought that if this wasn't the end of the world, it sure felt like it.

Alaska Earthquake 1964
Where were you?

ANCHORAGE

Yule Kilcher
A Sense of Community

I WAS SITTING IN THE LOBBY OF THE BARANOF HOTEL in Juneau waiting for a fellow senator to go with me to a late finance committee meeting; we were listening to Anchorage news on the radio close by.

A slight tremor rattled the furniture and the radio went dead. People on telephones to Anchorage looked stunned as the phones went silent. We all began to realize that something momentous must have taken place out west. Through amateur short-wave radio operators the disaster was communicated.

There was all over a great spirit of cooperation, a sense of community, something akin to exhilaration.

Several of us legislators contacted Governor Egan at the Mansion, and before daybreak the governor, with us western legislators, flew west in a noisy National Guard airplane, and were soon circling over smoking, burning, and half submerged Valdez, heading for Anchorage, seeing brown dust on the snowfields before Anchorage caused by mountainslides everywhere, seeing broken bridges along Turnagain Arm, wide cracks in the road and on the Anchorage airport. The town resembled a disturbed anthill; there was tremendous activity everywhere.

I was immediately involved in organizing traffic, assuming responsibility for removing road blocks to free roads, keeping traffic free for impending paving. Suntanned, uni-

167

Yule Kilcher

formed and armed Eskimo National Guardsmen with serious miens were patrolling the streets guarding the broken stores. There was all over a great spirit of cooperation, a sense of community, something akin to exhilaration.

Neil McArthur
A Trip Home

IN MARCH OF 1964 I WAS AT THE U.S. ARMY ENGINEER
SCHOOL, Fort Belvoir, Virginia, a few miles from
Washington, D.C., learning to make maps at the sug-
gestion of Uncle Sam. On Saturday the 28th I heard sketchy
news of an earthquake in Alaska. By Monday the papers
were reporting a death toll in the thousands and massive destruction.

Naturally I was very concerned about friends in my ad-
opted home, and called Senator Bob Bartlett's office. They
had only five names of earthquake victims at that time, but
one was Bill Taylor, father of the girl I wished to marry. I

Airport Control Tower   Neil McArthur

Neil McArthur

Denali Theater   Neil McArthur

immediately decided to fly to Alaska, so put in for an emergency leave, starting with the quick-witted sergeant in charge of my classes. He phoned the captain, saying "This guy's senator just called him...," and I was on my way.

Next morning my Pacific Northern Airlines flight touched down on the decidedly lumpy runway in Anchorage and taxied to a large shed which was serving as a passenger terminal. I believe it had been intended for Northern Consolidated's cargo.

Walking out the other side of the shed, I dropped my duffel bag in the open trunk of a waiting cab. The driver shot out of her seat as if she'd just spotted a snake under the gas pedal, and sighed relief that it wasn't another aftershock. I could only stammer an apology.

We splashed on into Spenard where I appeared unannounced at my friends' home. Bill Taylor was a quiet, capa-

170

Frame Houses   Neil McArthur

ble, unpretentious man who grew up north of Fairbanks, married young, and worked for the FAA as an air traffic controller at Lake Hood, later at Anchorage International.

According to a coworker who made it, they ran to escape the collapsing control tower, but a tall cabinet of recording tape fell on Bill and crushed him. His wife and daughter were devastated. Thirty years afterward I remember him with great respect, still think of things he said, things I'd like to ask him.

80CS

A week later I walked through the chuckholes and melting snow of Spenard Road, across Chester Creek and up Romig to Anchorage, taking a few photos along the way. The L Street Apartments, still in use today, were extensively cracked between the windows. A fellow who lived on the

Neil McArthur

I walked through the chuckholes and melting snow of Spenard Road, taking a few photos along the way top floor said he'd spent the three and a half minutes of the earthquake dodging his furniture while the room went by.

Much damage was caused by subsidence of waterlogged soil, and frame houses were tipped into holes, but otherwise appeared quite sound. Commercial structures fared less well, losing their facades as the J.C. Penney store did, or breaking over the edge of holes that suddenly appeared. Throughout downtown Anchorage, Eskimo Scouts directed traffic. Some of them apparently had better sense than to bother with talk. A friend who'd wanted to drive farther along a closed street quickly reversed when a Scout simply lowered his rifle right at the car.

D&D Cafe   Neil McArthur

A Trip Home

Several blocks of the north side of 4th Avenue subsided about one story, in the area now occupied by the Post Office Mall, Sunshine Mall, and Holiday Inn.
In its article about the '64 earthquake, National Geographic included a shot of a green felt-covered card table with spilled poker chips in the D&D Cafe. Buck Cassidy, the old sourdough with whom I'd once shared a cabin at 328½ E. Fourth Avenue, in what's now midair, played cards for the house at that table.
He allowed they'd made a record-breaking trip across the street to the Panhandle Bar when the quake hit! Of course, I returned to the Army, and life went on for the majority of us who survived. The obvious lessons are to avoid tall buildings, don't hang bookshelves over the bed, and don't believe what you read in the papers, but there are subtler messages.
Reminders that we are all transient, we are all vulnerable; that we should respect each other while we can, help each other while we are able.

... we should respect each other while we can, help each other while we are able

©1994 Neil McArthur

Anne Wieland
Remembering the Great Alaska Quake

O N THE AFTERNOON OF FRIDAY, MARCH 27, 1964, I was sewing curtains for our new house in Scenic Park in the east side of Anchorage. We had moved in just after Christmas 1963 when the house was completed. Leslie would be 3 in May and Linda was 15 months old. Leslie was holding scissors in her hand, cutting scraps of cloth. Linda was standing up in her playpen next to me and amusing herself by dropping her toys out of it. Their father was at his office at the old Presbyterian Hospital at 10th and L Street, having just joined the Alaska Clinic as a family practitioner two weeks earlier, after he had completed his tour with the Air Force. The radio was playing Beethoven's 6th symphony, the Pastorale, and the famous musical thunderstorm was in full sway.

Suddenly the sway spread to the immediate surroundings. I remember looking east across the Chugach mountains as the initial jolt and subsequent rolling of the earth grew stronger and stronger. It seemed that the motion was coming from that direction. I was no stranger to earthquakes by 1964, but this one was definitely more intense than any experienced before.

When our prize AM/FM short wave radio fell with a crash to the floor I decided it was time to get out of the house. Leslie was frozen in her tracks and couldn't get the scissors off her fingers. I grabbed her in one arm and swept Linda out of her playpen with the other, the scissors falling to the floor which was by now lurching from side to side. We staggered down the stairs of the split-level house. I

175

threw open the front door and watched as the glass door bent and made distorted reflections like a circus mirror as the intensity of the quake continued to increase. I stopped long enough to put Leslie down and pick up the evening paper and stick it inside the door.

Al, you're a geologist, DO SOMETHING!

Just as we stepped out onto the landing, the ground fell out of under us, swayed crazily, and subsided again. Somehow, we ended up a few feet from the door, lying face down in the snow, unable to stand up. I noticed our neighbor Al Wanek's garage door rolling up and down, and soon Al emerged. He was a long-time Alaskan who worked for the U.S. Geological Survey. He too was unable to stand. I yelled at him, "Al, you're a geologist, DO SOMETHING!!" The young birch trees swept like windshield wipers bending low to the ground first on one side then the other. Dogs were crying out in terror. The neighbor across the street emerged wild-eyed, clad in nothing but a towel.

The girls and I lay in the snow for what seemed like 4 or 5 minutes. From the corner of my eye I could see our house changing shape, from parallelogram to rectangle and back again. My mind skipped from fear to keen interest in all that was happening back to terror again. Gradually the jolting changed to a more predictable wave motion, such as one might experience in a boat in 3 foot seas. I tried to stand up, and actually saw the ground take the shape of swells moving toward us from the east. I stabilized myself and tried with all my might to steady the movement of the waves as one would try to steady a boat in the open water. I gripped the ground with such intensity that my thighs ached for days afterwards from the exertion.

Eventually the ground motion subsided to a point where I thought we could go back inside. When we did reenter, the power was out, not to be restored for 2 or 3 days. The kitchen was a mess. Bottles had fallen on the floor and smashed, the contents spilled everywhere and mixed with bits of broken glass and food that had fallen out of cabinets. Pictures were askew, and gouges appeared in arcs all around the chandeliers and around paintings on the wall. Some furniture had slid around the floor, and other objects had fallen down. The children were scared as aftershocks rocked us again.

The phone rang, a miraculous link with the outside world. It was a friend inquiring if we were OK and telling us that a portion of the new J.C. Penney building had fallen into the street and killed someone in downtown Anchorage.

After a while, my husband appeared and told us that he had to go back to the hospital because many people had been cut by flying glass. All physicians were being called back in to work until injuries had been tended. He told of gaps and crevasses in the roadbed on the difficult trip home. I felt abandoned as he drove away, but we had been invited next door to sleep at Al and Gerry's so that we didn't have to stay alone.

Al and Gerry had a radio that survived the quake. Because most or all the Anchorage stations were off the air, we were able to pick up the faint signal of radio station KING from Seattle. We heard the first reports of tremendous devastation in southcentral Alaska. At that time we did not know that their sources were incomplete and greatly exaggerated the impacts of the quake. We fully expected that Anchorage would experience a tsunami from the quake or aftershocks. I slept only fitfully that night.

Anne Wieland

Neighbors on the other side of us worked for IBM. Long distance communication was not possible after the quake, so we asked them to notify our parents in Pennsylvania and New Jersey through the company network that we had survived the quake and, other than perhaps $2000 damage to our house, were fine. Eventually word of our safety reached our parents. As it turned out, all over Alaska neighbors were helping neighbors. The quake knocked down some barriers and brought many people together, even as it had brought the state to its knees in a state of emergency.

We were without water and power and could not flush the toilet. It was cold inside because we were not allowed to use our fireplaces due to the frequency of large aftershocks. But we had a car, and the weather was rather mild with temperatures in the 20s. On Sunday, friends invited us on a most unusual post-earthquake outing. High up on O'Malley road some enterprising folks had started a business called "Trout Unlimited." They had built an earthen dam across a little stream, and in the resulting small lake, had introduced about 6000 or 7000 trout. One could hire a boat, catch trout, and then pay for them by the inch.

Unfortunately, the earthen dam had bust in the quake, and as the pond gushed out of its confines, it disgorged several thousand trout. As the surge of water flooded through the little creek valley that drained the lake, the trout were hung up in the willow bushes that crowded its banks. There they froze by the hundreds. We arrived, several adults and children with bags and baskets in hand, and had an uproarious time picking trout out of the bushes. We stopped only because we had no way to preserve the fish for more than a few days. Soon our cats became the main beneficiaries of our expedition.

Meanwhile, my parents were frantically trying to reach us from New Jersey as phone service had been restored. It was hard for them to believe that we had been out having a great time taking advantage of one of the consequences of the strongest earthquake of the century. My mother recounted that on the evening of March 27, at 10:27 Eastern Standard Time, that is, at exactly the moment that the quake hit, she had experienced a tremendous period of anxiety and had gone to see "who in the family had died on that day." Then she began to feel that something terrible had happened to me. So she was not surprised when the next morning she heard of the quake on the radio.

It's hard to believe that it has been 30 years since the quake. The recollections are very vivid, as though they had happened just yesterday. Leslie's earliest memory is of spending the night at the Waneks after the quake. Experiencing this quake has made others seem modest by comparison for me. But I still feel very uncomfortable in tall buildings in Anchorage, and am convinced that a Big One can come again. It is very disturbing that our memory of this event seems so short and that the lessons learned appear to be forgotten. People have built once again in some very unstable parts of Anchorage and elsewhere. The next time we may not be nearly as lucky as we were in 1964.

M. Walter Johnson
A Personal Account

AT 5:36 PM ON FRIDAY, MARCH 27, 1964, I was still in my office on the third floor of the Alaska Native Medical Center hospital building. Even though I had previously experienced minor earthquakes, I did not recognize the tremor and noise as one because of its extreme violence. The thought that came to my mind was that nearby Elmendorf Air Force Base was under attack.

After a few seconds, perhaps, of being shaken to and fro even in the very substantial building, I became concerned that the structure might collapse. So I hastened down the hall to the stairs and on down the steps, descending to the ground floor and out the nearest exit. Getting out of the building seemed to take a long time as I was hurled from one side of the stair well to the other on the way out.

The thought that came to my mind was that nearby Elmendorf Air Force Base was under attack

At, or very near the time I arrived outside the building, the major tremor stopped. By then I realized the event was, in fact, an earthquake.

The silence was overwhelming. I recalled the account an old Alaskan prospector in Wiseman had given me years before of the 1906 San Francisco earthquake. He emphasized the fires. I thought of broken gas lines, electrical "shorts" and disrupted furnaces. I waited to see the city go up in flames. But it did not. Again, it was the silence and absence of activity that impressed me.

181

M. Walter Johnson

Olson architectural firm in Juneau, Alaska, had designed the hospital building, which is in the shape of a cross, so each wing could structurally separate at its junction with the center core and roll individually with minimal damage to the whole. Patients on the fifth floor of the building reported seeing a gap they estimated up to one foot [wide] open as the wings separated from the central building.

It was not yet dark so the loss of electrical power was less of a crisis than it might have been until auxiliary generators came into play. After seeing that none of the patients appeared to be injured, I drove home to check on the family. The most distinct memory of that trip was seeing the many fissures in the road. However, none [were] so large as to prevent passage.

Both the maintenance and medical staff reported to the hospital. My recollection is that the emergency was managed in an orderly manner as the damage was assessed. The ground, along with the birch trees standing on the bluff to the north of the hospital had broken away and subsided so that only the tops of those trees remained in view.

The ground on which the hospital stood was declared high risk for future earthquakes. However, no action was taken to replace the medical center on more stable ground until almost three decades had passed. Who knows if the building will go over the bluff with the next earthquake?

Debra Williams
Wrath of God

O N MARCH 27, 1964, I WAS IN OUR APARTMENT
on Fort Richardson Army base. Earlier I had been
playing outdoors until a schoolmate yelled out her
window "What do you think you're doing? Don't you know
this is Good Friday; you should be inside praying!" I had
no idea what Good Friday was but I hurried inside grabbed
my younger sister and began to pray. I certainly did not wish
to incur the wrath of God. You can imagine my confusion
when that evening we seemed to have incurred his wrath
anyway.

When the quake started, my older sister was frying pota-
toes for dinner while we younger kids watched TV in the
basement. We had heard about tremors before but had
never felt one so when it started we were excited to finally
feel a "tremor." Our excitement quickly turned to panic as
we headed upstairs. We had lived in Kansas before and my
sis had been told in case of tornado to get us kids into the
basement. She assumed that must be a safe place so hurried
us all back downstairs. We learned later that the basement is
not necessarily the best place to be in a quake.

My #2 sister got caught on **... as the floor cracked**
the stairway frozen in fear. She **and the washer, dryer**
could neither go up nor down **and freezer bounced**
and cans and bottles stored on
shelves at the head of the stairs **around the room like**
were crashing on and around **popcorn popping.**
her. The rest of us were spread-
eagled on the concrete floor of the basement watching in

horror as the floor cracked and the washer, dryer and freezer bounced around the room like popcorn popping. When the shaking began to subside some I made my way up the stairs through all the glass and rubble and pried my sister's fingers off the banister and drug her down the stairs. We all huddled together scared out of our wits. A few minutes later a stranger came in the house calling out to see if everyone was OK. When he learned our parents were not home he told us to go get in a car—any car—in the lot and stay there windows up, doors closed, till our parents could get to us and not to move from there no matter what. We did as told.

My mom spent the quake huddled under a counter at the PX with her workmates. My dad had just come from the NCO Club and could not quite figure why the road was responding so badly to his driving so he pulled off and only then realized the ground was moving.

Fortunately, the housing on base was quite sturdy and we didn't get quite the shock that Anchorage did. Other than the cracks here and there and the huge mess left from broken bottles throughout the house and the fridge and cupboards that had dumped their contents, we got off pretty well.

I do remember walking back into the apartment seeing the food flung all over the kitchen and wondering, "who's going to clean up this mess?" My mom immediately rolled up her sleeves gave us each a trash bag and a room, set the example for us and that question was quickly answered.

To this day I am mortified when the earth shifts and when the movie *Earthquake* came out, it was one I chose to pass up.

©1994 Debra Williams

Al Clayton, Sr.
At Crosswind Lake

I WAS OFF WORK AT 4:00 PM, AFTER AN 8 HOUR SHIFT at Copper Valley Electric Diesel Power Plant at Glennallen, Alaska. The idea was to get to Crosswind Lake, about 17 miles north of mile 170 Glenn Highway, for a weekend of fishing for lake trout. My snow plane, a three ski, propeller driven machine, was already loaded on the trailer and we, my friend Markle Ewan Jr. and I, drove to mile 170 Glenn Highway, unloaded and headed for the lake without incident. We wanted to get some holes cut through the ice, which was more than 4 feet thick, for fishing before dark.

The first hole was almost chiseled through when a jolt hit us and the ice began to crack in all directions. The snow plane was but a few feet away, and with its front ski (8 ft 6 in. long) to jump on, it looked like the thing to do. Markle said, "I'm going to the gravel beach" (about 200 ft. away). For him there was about three feet of open water to get across.

For an eternity it seemed, it kept shaking, most of five minutes. The tops of the spruce trees on shore were waving together and then apart because of ground motion. A coyote down the beach a ways, came out of the timber and headed across the ice at full speed. He went nearly across the part of the lake, saw something and made a 90 degree left turn, and headed straight north. As for me, I was holding on to the snow plane, standing on the spring loaded front ski holding on with both hands.

Al Clayton, Sr.

When we moved across the lake to go to our cabin to camp that night, cracks in the thick ice showed the water was squeezed out of the crack and had fallen in the snow alongside. Across from our fishing spot on the east side of the lake, the ice was broken with its edges sticking up. The next day, March 28th, we had not caught a lake trout. Jack Wilson, a pilot from Gulkana airport, flew in to drop me a message. On about his 3rd pass by the cabin, a wet monkey glove was dropped with a note in it that said to come back to the Glennallen Power Plant as soon as I could. I found out the plant had been down for five hours.

Martine Clayton
Events In Glenallen

EARLIER IN 1964, BEFORE THE GREAT EARTHQUAKE, there was a wind warning of one hundred miles per hour. When the secretary of Copper Valley Electric rang our company home phone, she said the children would be brought home early on the school buses. I asked if the timing was accurate because warnings about Hurricane Hazel in New York in 1954 when Al and I got married were about half an hour behind that storm. To me the children were safer at school than in a bus with 100 mph winds blowing.

...the crack that ran under the house and right under us kept opening and closing...

There was time to gather an "activity box" and a "snack box" in the hall where the bedroom doors and the bathroom door closed to make a safe haven from flying glass if wind knocked out a window. The secretary called back to tell me which way the wind was blowing. By then I had watched the direction the flocks of snow birds were taking through our yard.

Earthquakes don't usually give any warnings. Sometimes the seismic activity can warn of coming volcanic action as with some of the volcanoes like Mt. Redoubt that can blow ash to Homer, where we have lived since 1988.

Usually the earthquakes last a matter of seconds rather than minutes. When the great quake hit about 5:30 pm, March 27, 1964, it didn't stop, so we went to our safe haven in the hallway by the bedrooms. Three of the children made it there on their own. Our oldest daughter, Marsha—a third grader in school—was trying to get to us from her bedroom.

She couldn't make it on her own because the motion of the house had the piano, a spinet size, rolling out from the wall. I went in to get her and then we all sat down on the floor together in the hall. I had a daughter in the crook of each elbow. My little son stood between my legs and hung on to my neck. Jeanette, our second daughter—a first grader—held my fingertips, as she was near my feet.

To add to our panic the plant alarm bell rang with the volume of a school fire bell. This bell was above our heads and would wake Al to indicate trouble at the power plant nearby when Copper Valley Electric didn't have a person on night shift.

The Clayton Family

My voice volume was louder than the bell as I pleaded with God for mercy and care. Then the crack that ran under the house and right under us kept opening and closing, I realized we might be in our final day on God's good earth. I wondered if that crack split the floor would I be able to hang on to all four of the children.

So to face eternity, I quieted my voice volume, and together we shared the scriptures the children knew — John 3:16, Psalm 23, and the Lord's prayer. (Seems like we had just returned from Good Friday services at Glennallen Community Chapel when all the shaking, quaking started.)

Figuring that if the quake was so powerful 115 miles inland from the sea (Glennallen to Valdez), it must be terrible by the ocean. We prayed for friends in Anchorage. God answers prayers. Though houses slipped on three sides of them, they were safe and the father joined them later in the day after his quake–shake experience in downtown Anchorage.

Each time the crack opened and closed, dust and dirt came up from under the house through the cold air vent there in the hall. That was a bother and I wondered if I should move the children or take them outside. That thought was balanced with how could I keep track of all four of the children. (Later descriptions indicated the ground rolled in about five foot waves.)

What a relief when all the quaking–shaking stopped. My neighbor came to see if we were okay. My reply —"Yes... You get where it's safe before another one hits!" She had given me a casserole which was in the oven for supper.

Her husband was on duty at the power plant and said later he, too, thought it was the end of our earth. He'd worked the big tankers in high seas so had a valid comparison for the various actions of our planet.

Cleanup! The bathroom door wouldn't open very far— everything off all shelves and out of the medicine closet. Best place to start was the kitchen to get to the casserole. What a mess—broken dishes mixed with eggs that came out of the refrigerator and scrambled on the floor. A couple wedding plates saved—resting in the teatowel drawer that rolled out and caught them. The everyday dishes were just fine—rode the quake out in the drainer in the sink.

There went the alarm again! Another earthquake? No. But the children scrambled to the hall without direction from me. Like Pavlov's dogs, trained by the bell. Alfred had fallen asleep on the couch, but Jeanette woke him up and helped him get down the hall. Through tears she apologized for waking him. I think we were all close to tears from our frightful experience.

The power plant wasn't quite ready to go back on line then but later we had power. The experienced operator had crawled around and shut every thing down when the quake started or we would have been without power longer.

When my dear neighbor came back, she helped me restore the bedroom to some semblance of order and we arranged everything so we could all sleep in one bedroom. I had told the kids to "tinkle" on the garage floor—an all dirt floor (could be scooped out later.) Once I had gradually dragged enough stuff out through the small space the bathroom door would open and cleaned that area up, we felt all was getting back to normal.

The manager arrived to go through the house with me. When we went to the garage, I wondered about my decision to let the children use the dirt floor out there. A pound of oleo was under one of the tires on the station wagon. The car had shot backwards into the garage door and had done its share of going back and forward on its own.

When the relief operator came on duty he brought his younger son with him. When his dad worked, our guest slept on the couch. They had watched a lake near their home churn to icy pieces. They were concerned just as much about the oldest brother who was out ice fishing with my Al at Crosswind Lake. The manager told me that they would send for Al.

KCAM at Central Alaska Mission (now Send International) had been gearing up to give us our first radio station. They received permission to start broadcasting on an emergency temporary basis. We were feeling more secure. Al and his friend got home Saturday instead of Sunday, which had been the original plan. Were we ever glad to see the boys.

Repair time started. Our house was a bit twisted; the front door wouldn't close. We've been grateful that the steel I-beams kept the house together even though they were shaken off the concrete support posts by the time the quake was over.

As the workmen started jacking on the house, the younger two at home would call to me. Then I would go visiting so they didn't have to experience the vibrations again. One day Shirley had her little brother Alfred and her dolls gathered in the rocking chair with her arms around all and her hands over their mouths. She was four years old at this point and Alfred would be two that May. When I asked her what she was doing, her reply was, "You ought to know, Mother. I'm keeping the dirt out of their mouths." Play therapy is wonderful healer.

What did I learn from that **We live in Homer, the** tremendous earthquake experi- **most beautiful place** ence? I want to be helpful to others as my good neighbor **on earth.** was that day. She'd made beautiful birthday cakes for each of my children, but on earthquake day she was like a saint to me. The biggest lesson was to remember to live each day so we're ready to meet our MAKER at a moment's notice. We are well BLESSED. The four children and their families live in

Martine Clayton

Alaska. We count twelve grandchildren. We live in Homer, the most beautiful place on earth.

Marie Doyle
The Once and Future Earthquake Park

IT IS 5:20, MARCH 27, 1964. I have just picked up Dave after his piano lesson. Driving west on Northern Lights Boulevard, I take a right on Telequana, a left on Clay Products and pull into the driveway of our home on the corner of Clay Products and Chilligan Drive. I leave the car out of the garage because my husband, Barney, and I are going out to the Greens for dinner. It is a dinner party I will never make.

Dave and I walk around the house to the front door. It is peaceful. We can smell a wood fire from Grace and Ken Johnson's fireplace across the road.

We walk up the flagstones and in the front door. "Hi Annie, we're home." Annie is in bed with the measles, but no, here she comes now in her little blue bathrobe. She is seven.

"Can I have a drink of water, Mama?"

I hand her her drink, "Feeling better, Honey?"

After her drink she says, "Yes," and comes over for a hug just as Dave comes in to ask me how to spell the word "inverse."

"You know where the dictionary is..."

WHAM!

I grab both children and stagger to the front door.

The leg of lamb I'm roasting for the children's dinner is skidding across the kitchen floor. Big beams creak as the fireplace lifts six inches out of the floor and sinks six inches below.

Marie Doyle

We are huddled under the massive lintel over the front door. Ann is whimpering.

"Stay with me. We're okay," I lie. We watch the Johnsons' house tilt to a 40 degree angle, shuddering, crackling as the new cedar siding splinters and snaps. Around it, 30 foot spruce trees are sucked out of sight. I know we are goners. Off to the right, Chilligan Drive crumbles down a

Mud cones in future Earthquake Park   Conrad Bitter

newly forming cliff. Where there had been houses and forested hills is now gray, churning mud and beyond, the sea.

Gushes of mud spurt 20 feet into the air. To the left, Clay Products [street] is gone. The horror I experience now will be in future known as Earthquake Park. I see Barney home from work trying to crawl up the path. He is not moving. We are rooted to the place we are standing.

Only the earth moves, growling and undulating. Our house groans, I glance back in the entry way where a Lennox vase is dancing on the polished slate floor. How it came out of the sideboard in the dining room, God only knows.

194

The Once and Future Earthquake Park

Turning, I see, on the remnant of Chilligan Drive, seven neighborhood children running, falling, crawling on hands and knees, screaming in terror as the road falls away behind them. Now all the houses across the road are gone. The houses on our side are going now.

Five houses away from us. Four away. The Shohls' house, three away ...

Silence. One more tree sinks out of view beyond the cliff, heaving a spurt of mud in its place.

... children running, falling, crawling on hands and knees, screaming in terror as the road falls away behind them.

"What was that, Mama?" sobs Annie.

"An earthquake," says 11 year old Dave.

We begin to breathe again. To move.

Grace Johnson clambers out of her tilted house to meet Barney, the children and me in the middle of what remains of Chilligan Drive.

For the first time I feel my unborn baby stir inside me.

Julia Person
These are the Times

WHILE GROWING UP, I always thought that some-day I would have a pilot's license and would keep a plane next to my house in case of an earth-quake. I hear people say, "Oh, an earthquake is no worse than hurricanes or tornadoes," but I lived where there were tornadoes and there were warnings and "hidey holes" to climb into. Same with hurricanes. An earthquake gives no warning. The experts say, "Stay inside, under a door jamb." Easily said, but the house I was in fell apart. Houses in 1964 broke in half and crumpled. So you run outside; but the foundation of our lives, the earth, is no longer trustwor-thy—it can open up and swallow you. The only safety I could figure out was to get up into the air.

I was a child when the earthquake hit. I've never com-pared my memories of that day to the recollections of the adults involved. The children I was with remember nothing. When I tell my story the terror of that time is with me. I may not have all the facts right, but here is my story as I know it.

I was 8½ years old in March, 1964. When the quake hit, I was in the Anchorage suburb called Turnagain By The Sea, the place now called Earthquake Park. My younger sister, who was 5, my younger brothers, ages 3 and 1, and I were staying with friends while my parents were in San Francisco. It had been a traumatic time for my family. Six weeks ear-lier, my mother had been in a car accident while taking my sister and other children to kindergarten. A drunk driver had swerved across the road and hit my mother's car head on. The front seat lifted up as the cars hit. My mother reached over to protect my youngest brother, riding on the passenger side. Both of them had gone through the windshield. One side of my mother's face was crushed and my brother suffered head trauma. My sister was not injured, but seeing my mother covered in blood, she'd become hysterical. Now my mother had healed enough to go to San Francisco with my father to seek a reconstructive surgeon. It must have been difficult to leave her children in the care of others, but it was impossible for us to accompany them.

My older brother was staying with another family in Turnagain, the Tikkas. The rest of us were left in the care of Brooke and Wilda Marston. The Marstons lived in a beautiful log home. As children we were enamored with it. There was a huge log swing set in the front yard and a wonderful playhouse in the back, looking over the inlet. Inside there was a wrought iron spiral staircase connecting the first and second floor. Of course we always wanted to slide down the banister, but that was forbidden.

On the day of the earthquake, my older brother was on a ski trip to Alyeska with the Tikkas. The Marstons' daughter, Blythe, had gone too. The youngest Tikka children, ages 5, 3, and 1 and Erin Marston, 3, were with us. At 5:30 we sat on the floor of the playroom, in our pajamas, watching "The Buckaroo Club" on television. A Rocky and Bullwinkle cartoon was on, and Mr. Peabody was talking when suddenly the TV went blank. Erin walked to the set and gave it a wallop when the ground began to shake. Then the ground gave way. The house tilted and shook. We froze. Wilda screamed, "Erin! Erin!" and we all rushed to the stairwell. "Slide down," she said, "Slide down! Hurry!" One by one the children slid down the banister. I think at that point I was frightened more that Wilda would tell us to break a steadfast rule, than I was by the continued movement of the house. I realize now that when the adults acted out of character, I was most afraid. As I prepared to go down the banister, I looked back into the playroom. Two floor to ceiling cabinets at the end of the room began to slide across the floor, moving quickly toward the place where we children had been sitting. With that view I slid down the banister.

The house which had seemed so solid only a few minutes ago was breaking up. Creaking and groaning, the logs were being pulled in different directions. **Where the backyard had been was a small strip of land and a bluff to the water.** It was clear we could not stay in the house. Telling us to grab our coats in the hall, Wilda had a blanket and herded us out into the yard. What a sight we saw. The playhouse was gone, swept into the Inlet. Where the backyard had been was a small strip of land and a bluff to the water.

Spreading the blanket, Wilda had us all sit down, and then went back into the house. As the oldest, I think I tried to comfort the others. In thinking back, I know my sister was in shock. She'd had too much trauma, and cried continually. All of us were crying as Wilda came back out of the house bringing our boots if she could find them, coats and blankets. She also brought a loaf of bread and some jam. She settled us down as best she could and opening the bread bag, began spreading jam on each slice. It's funny what is clear in my memories. I can see my slippers — fake cowboy boots made of cow-spotted fleece. I remember looking at the Sunrise bread and how ordinary the blue and white checkered bag looked with the jam jar next to it as Wilda calmly spread jam on slice after slice of bread. Sitting on the blanket it seemed we were having a nice picnic, except our setting was extraordinary. One of the Tikka boys looked as his bread and said, "But Wilda, you know I don't like jam."

As we sat there tremor after tremor came and the ground would open and close around us. We cried that we were cold and wanted to go back into the house, but Wilda said it wasn't safe. Looking at the house, we believed her. It sat askew, tilted ridiculously on parts of the foundation, all dignity gone. The swing set in the front yard was far away, on top of a tall bluff. The ground under the house had collapsed and we had ridden a landslide to our current resting spot. Wilda assured us that someone would come to help us and that we just needed to stay calm.

Then the ground shifted again, noisily crushing the car as the crevasse closed. I don't remember how she managed to keep us warm and entertained. I recall during one tremor, the ground under the driveway opened up and we watched the big Plymouth slide slowly backward into the crevasse. Then the ground shifted again, noisily crushing the car as the crevasse closed. "I never liked that car," Wilda said.

A woman came by dressed in her bathrobe and carrying her small spaniel under one arm. Wilda urged her to wait with us for rescue but she wouldn't and wandered off. It was a world turned upside down. Everywhere you looked, the trees that once were a forest now stood on blocks of frozen ground tilting at various unlikely angles. How Wilda maintained calm I do not know. I think that I am now about the age she was then, and the idea of caring for eight young children during such an ordeal is overwhelming. But she kept us calm, and finally a helicopter came and hovered overhead. Through the open door men leaned out, shouting at us, asking if we were okay. They lowered a rope ladder but Wilda, and perhaps I, were the only ones who could have made it up. After shouting back and forth, it was decided that one man would come down to us and help us walk out.

I remember him coming down the ladder. And I remember all of us being frightened at the thought of climbing out. The bluff seemed too far, and there was nothing but rubble and fallen trees between us and it. And the tremors continued intermittently. As the oldest daughter of five children, I was used to being in charge of the younger ones. I think that he talked to me and said as the oldest I would have to set an example for the others, but maybe that was just my mother's voice in my head. I was angry at my sister for not helping and for crying so much. When we said we couldn't do it, he told us the story of the little engine that could.

"Say it with me," he said, "I think I can! I think I can!" "I think I can," we cried doubtfully, "I think I can." He took an infant in his arm and a 3 year old by the hand. Wilda did the same. And we set out.

We climbed over fallen trees, climbed through gullies of frozen ground, and were finally near the base of the bluff. Then a tremor hit. Near us the ground opened. My sister slipped into the crevasse. The man hurried to the edge and grabbed her to pull her out and the crevasse began to close. Harder he pulled and faster it closed, and when it closed with a snap, her bunny slipper was caught tightly in the earth. Days later my father tried to pry it out of the ground without success.

Climbing the bluff was difficult. I don't know how high it was, my older brother says 50 feet, but I know we had to go under and over fallen trees, over loose ground and frozen ground, and it seemed insurmountable. The cries of "I think I can," had grown faint, and we children were giving up.

Julia Person

Then we heard shouts from the top of the bluff! There was my older brother! The Tikkas were there and Brooke Marston. Seeing our friends and families gave us all the added momentum we needed and we made it to the top. We were hurried to the Tikka's house. Before the quake it was a couple of streets over, but now it was right by us. A fire had been built in the fireplace, and we were given dry clothing and something warm to drink. One of the children had a birthday soon, and the talk was of his birthday cake which had fallen from its place on top of the refrigerator and broken up. "It's an earthquake cake," we all laughed and laughed, but it wasn't that funny.

The adults did their best to make the whole thing seem an adventure. While I am sure they were aware of the most terrifying aspects, they protected us as best they could. Later, as we sat in the darkness, eating cold cuts by candle light, the police came. Shining their flashlights around, they informed us that a tsunami was coming, and we needed to get to higher ground. Quickly we were bundled up and ushered into the cars. I ended up in Brooke's station wagon. Northern Lights Boulevard was the only way out of that area of town in those days, so the road was clogged with people in cars and people walking. In their arms were belongings and children. My memory of that night, as we sought to outrun the oncoming water, was like the scene in a Godzilla movie, when the families are desperately fleeing the city. I believe we saw people with no vehicles pounding on the passing cars, begging for help, but we had no room in our car filled with children and adults. My brother doesn't recall this, but he was in a different car. It is vividly etched in my mind, because I wondered what would happen to all those people.

These are the Times

When we got out of town, we headed to a friend's house, the home of Alex and Muriel Combs. I recall once we got there, Muriel took charge of us kids, talking to us, singing and settling us in for the night. The other adults seemed to disappear. Alex told me recently that they all had a stiff drink, but I do not know. The stress of maintaining a semblance of calm for us children must have been exhausting.

As we slept, my parents in San Francisco were trying desperately to find out what had happened. Obviously, telecommunications were not what they are today. First they heard that all of Anchorage was gone. Then that was revised to say only the Turnagain area was lost. Telephone communication was down, radios were trying to get back on the air, all flights were canceled with the airport and military airfields damaged. They were scheduled to fly out of San Francisco the next morning and were determined to go as far as they could. The flight into Seattle was delayed, but they were told that the flight to Anchorage was rerouted to Fairbanks. They only had 15 minutes to catch it. Mother remembers running across the tarmac, desperate to be on board that flight. She says that she and my father never talked during the entire flight. She says that she was afraid to say anything because all she could think of were things too frightening to say.

After landing in Fairbanks, the passengers were told the Anchorage airport was open. Next to Mother sat a woman who talked incessantly about her fears about her family in Anchorage. As the plane approached Anchorage, and my father looked out the window. He saw Turnagain, and knew at that moment that we were certainly dead. No one could have survived that. He didn't know how to tell Mother, so he stayed silent. Meanwhile Mother was promising the woman that they would take her to her family. When the plane landed, they ran for the parking attendant. Apparently in those days you left your car keys hanging on a wall. All the keys had fallen and were in a jumbled pile in a box. Mother recalls my father tearing through that box, searching for their key. Finally he found it, went to their car, and they drove the woman to her family. Then they turned toward Turnagain, only to find that the roads into the subdivision were blocked. Not knowing what else to do, they turned to Brooke's realty office.

Mother opened the door and there we were—roasting hot dogs over a hibachi! They were so relieved, but we refused to leave Wilda, and moved to huddle against her. Mother says that at first she was hurt, but then she realized that Wilda had saved us, and in all the uncertainty, Wilda was the person we trusted to take care of us. Mother joined us to roast hot dogs, and after a while we were ready to go home.

I heard later that the man who had helped us said that before our rescue he had not been convinced of the existence of God. He told of flying over the rubble and destruction of Turnagain, seeing all the land turned and twisted and torn. In the midst of this there was a tiny patch of level ground. On that patch was a blanket, and on that blanket were eight small children, and he believed.

Mary Lee Phillips
Dear Friends and Relatives

Dear Friends and Relatives,[†]

   Sincere and grateful thanks to all of you who sent reassuring calls, wires, and letters expressing concern over our welfare, at the time of the quake. After the earthquake (A.Q., as we say), it has taken a good part of each day to try to get back to normal living, and we couldn't find time to write the details. Compared to many people, our losses were almost nothing. Home and office are almost the same as before, with only a few more cracks in our house. None of us were injured—just shaken! Actually, we weren't frightened, until seeing and hearing of all the destruction in Anchorage, the other Alaskan coastal towns and villages, (and extending down to Crescent City, California). There are still jolts which freeze one in apprehension, and lesser tremors (two mild ones last night), which the seismologists tell us will continue for a while.

   Back to Good Friday, March 27th, 5:30 pm. Jane and Susan had returned from work ... **several houses had gone into the inlet ...** and school. I was making a few late preparations for dinner and Easter. Suddenly the house jerked, jumped and swayed. Glassware fell from the glass cabinet and smashed to bits. Food and medicine fell from cupboards. The three of us lurched to the center hallway and hung on to a wall.

[†]Submitted by Susan Phillips Cushing

Mary Lee Phillips

As it became worse, we decided to put on wraps and get out of the house. Outside, the road was waving and tree tops bending almost to the ground. Other people were out in the street, calling and yelling to each other. The girls ran around to the steps leading down to the first level, when a boy came running down the street, shouting to them to get away from the bluff—that several houses had gone into the inlet! We walked up that way to see what had happened.

Miraculously, the people had climbed out of their houses before they collapsed, or were heaved up and down in the huge chunks and cracks of earth. Evelyn Martin, a doctor's wife, was coming down the road, carrying a fur stole and an old apron. Her main concern was for her two children who hadn't returned home from skiing. Word of their safety wasn't received until the next day, but apparently Evelyn wasn't giving a second thought to her luxurious home which was lost. Two men were carrying an older woman to a place of safety. There were electric wires hanging down in the streets and deep cracks all around, and we went no closer to the broken off bluff until days later. We heard that all the homes in west Turnagain were gone also and no one knew how many lives! We felt we must find Francis and we went home for the car, which our next door neighbor had jacked around straight in the garage, and started down one street. Because of a large crack in that street we tried another and made our way to the office.

We found Francis safe and calm. The office was dark but otherwise the same, except for magazines and bottles scattered on the floor. Francis gathered some supplies and containers for water to take home and we started back. The police stopped us at Spenard Road saying that no one could go into the Turnagain area as a tidal wave was reported on the way. They advised us to go stay with friends. Jane was

206

Dear Friends and Relatives

worried about one of her friends and her little boy. We drove out to her house. Another couple and a man from Seward were there. Her husband was out helping the National Guard. Barbara distributed blankets but the guests shivered, slept little, and listened all night to the reports coming in on the transistor radio.

We resigned ourselves to the fact that our house, cat, and prized personal possessions would be swept away with the tidal wave, as the tide normally comes in below our house. However, the tidal wave spent its fury on the poor little towns of Valdez, Seward, Chenega, and Kodiak, never reaching here. Barbara found out the next day that her grandfather in Seward was drowned when the wave hit Seward. After a breakfast of cereal and milk and coffee made with snow melted over canned heat, we went home. By morning, police were allowing those who had homes remaining in the Turnagain area to go back.

The Army, Air Force, Civil Defense, Red Cross, Salvation Army, National Guard, utility companies, health and city agencies of all kinds quickly went into action. Power was restored on Saturday. Those with oil furnaces had heat. We converted back to oil from gas after heating by fire in the fireplace for ten days. The heat warmed our bodies and things began to look up! One of Susan's friends stayed with us. Her mother, Mrs. Alaska, was in Florida participating in the Mrs. America contest. The girls piled covers on their beds. I dragged a mattress near the fire. Francis slept on the couch and we took turns feeding wood to the fire. There was plenty of food in the house.

Mary Lee Phillips

Homes, food, wood for fuel, everything anyone needed was shared ...

For a month we cooked on two electric skillets. Water came first from the office, then from the purifying water trucks, which purified water and stored it in tanks, set up by the Army for people's use. Then, the city contracted for a company to set up, above ground, pipes all over the city to which home owners connect by hose. Now, after a month, we are back to gas for hot water and cooking purposes. Buildings are being repaired and rebuilt, but it will all take a very long time.

One wonderful thing is how everyone helped each other. Homes, food, wood for fuel, everything anyone needed was shared. Francis held open house evenings to give typhoid shots to the neighbors who didn't have time to stand in line at the health clinics. In return, one of our neighbors hooked us on to the water pipe supply furnishing his house, etc.

There are so many stories—some rumors—which people share when they meet in the stores, streets; some hilarious, and some too tragic. The most tragic was that two children of Dr. and Mrs. Mead were never found. Memorial services have been held for them. Dr. Mead helped take care of others at the hospital for a while, though later he went into a coma. The attorney mentioned in the color edition of Life magazine was a good friend of ours. Magazines give a good account of the destruction, but it gives the impression that the loss was almost total. There are still blocks and blocks of good, usable buildings and homes still standing. Business is getting started again. The railroads and highway to Seward are to be rebuilt but one can't drive there until about the middle of June. The economic picture isn't too bright, even with all the federal aid.

Dear Friends and Relatives

Our home area is classified as "unstable," but we are staying, as are some who live in the "hazard" area. Many have moved to safer ground or left Alaska for a time, or permanently. Some sent their children out to relatives or friends for school. Susan's school is not usable and they go on shift with East High. One school was used to house 300 Aleuts from Old Harbor and Chenega when their villages were swept away with the tidal wave. Some of them had slept in the hills until rescued.

It could have been worse for Anchorage. There were no large fires, nor tidal waves. People are accepting their plight dauntlessly—just grateful to be alive! In five minutes, lives were changed. One thing was revealed—that we are helpless against the forces of nature, and that we are not the rulers of our lives nor the universe!

Sincerely,

The Phillips Family

Daisy Lee Bitter
Dear Family and Friends

2804 Breezewood Drive
Anchorage, Alaska 99503
Friday, April 3, 1964
Dear Family and Friends[†],
   First, thanks for all the caring letters and offers of help.
They meant so much!
   Mentally, I've tried to gather my thoughts so many
times, but I can't seem to get them organized. If they're
somewhat jumbled, it is only a reflection of recent earth-
shaking events.
   Where do I start?
   It was Good Friday, March 27, just one week ago today.
Fortunately, schools were closed and I had taken Tim down-
town to see the Easter Egg Contest displays. We parked on
D Street between the Camera Center (Glenn and Ruth
McLain's store on 4th Avenue) and Penney's on 5th Avenue.
The Anchorage Sears Store, which Connie manages, is less
than a block away and across 5th Avenue from Penney's.
After meeting Connie for coffee and taking Tim to see sev-
eral of the displays, we left that area of Anchorage where so
much damage was destined to occur only minutes later.

[†] The following is a letter that Daisy Lee Bitter wrote to concerned
   friends and relatives shortly after the Great Alaskan Earthquake.
   Their son Tim is now 33 years old.

We headed for our home near Spenard Lake and stopped at the supermarket in Spenard to stock up on some groceries for Easter. At 5:34 PM we had just purchased dinner rolls at the bakery counter. A minute later it started like any other tremor to which we were accustomed.

Soon, however, canned vegetables began shooting off the shelves at us and fluorescent light fixtures started crashing down around us. Obviously, it was time to evacuate, so I grabbed Tim's hand and we joined the without-panic exodus to the parking lot. The ground was heaving convulsively by this time and we had some difficulty getting away from the building, for I had no intention of staying anywhere near the sidewalk in front of that phalanx of 12 foot high glass windows which ironically proclaimed "Safeway."

McLain's Camera Center

To stand up outside, we tried to hold on to cars, but the cars wouldn't hold still. An overhead parking lot light dropped like a bomb on a car hood nearby, so we staggered away from other overhead threats although it was more difficult to move than it was to stand erect, for there were deep potholes filled with melt water in the 4 to 6 inch deep ice layers that had hardened on the mall parking lot. A hundred feet away one of our neighbors, a Safeway cashier, got drenched as this rolling monster tumbled her into one of the wet, chilly potholes. We wanted to help but couldn't get to her. The ground kept undulating and rolling. Wasn't it ever going to stop? Was this phenomenon something greater than an earthquake? What could that be? This was not solid, steady terra firma any more—lots of "terra" and not "firma" at all.

Tree split by quake

Since Tim was only three years old, I didn't want him to catch the contagious panic that was rapidly spreading to some of the people around us. Several people were crying in fear. I encouraged Tim to observe closely so he could describe later the roller coaster ground that wouldn't hold still and the trees that were whipping sideways like inverted feather dusters on flexible fiberglass fishing poles.

Incredibly our world still kept rolling. Was all of our planet doing this? Had the earth's crust turned to Jello? Were we spinning off our axis? I had been in lots of earth-

Daisy Lee Bitter

J.C. Penney's

quakes before both in California and Alaska but they didn't last long. Why didn't this one stop?

The manager of the three Anchorage area Safeway stores was standing between us and the store. Concrete blocks flew out of the outside corners. He watched in disbelief as this invisible monster beneath us tried to rip his store apart.

The convulsive rolling finally stopped. We waited briefly in disbelief to see if it was really over. That was the longest five minutes of our lives! More adrenaline was secreted in Alaska during that time than in all the rest of North America!

Without groceries, we headed home. Our neighbors were in the street, very happy to see that we were all right. We checked the inside of the house. Some giant vandal had created a gigantic mess. On the kitchen floor was a "tossed salad." The ingredients were: rice, butter, mayonnaise, catsup, vinegar from cupboards on one side spiced with Con-

214

nie's coin collection and our stamp collection from the cupboards on the opposite side of the kitchen. Broken glass was
sprinkled throughout. Uprooted plants and dirt dotted the
living room rug. Downstairs, my previously organized files
were scrambled and the broken glass and splinters from
what had been a gun cabinet littered the other side of the
basement.

After surveying the interior damage we went outside to
compare notes with our neighbors. The damage didn't look
too severe in Spenard, but then our neighbor, Lloyd Slagle
drove in. He was still shaking, for he had been on the 4th
floor of the badly damaged Penney's. Luck was with him
that day. He was able to use the back stairs. He carried one
hysterical woman out and returned to where he saw two
legs sticking out from under a pile of rubbish. He helped
this woman out, too. Then Lloyd ran all the way around
Penney's to the front of the store where his car was parked.

Fourth Avenue

New bluff edge

The woman in the car ahead of him was fatally injured by the prestressed concrete slabs that peeled off the front of the building and crushed her car. Lloyd's car was unharmed.

Our concerns quickly turned to the people who weren't there, for until Lloyd related the devastation he saw as he tried to find a new way home we had no idea how bad it was elsewhere. Lloyd felt sure that several hundred people must have been killed and he told about all the destruction—even in the residential neighborhoods. The fourteen story apartment buildings had giant "X" cracks and looked twisted. Big homes were sinking into wide fissures.

Since Sears was within a half block of Penney's, we were all relieved to see Connie drive in! Since it had been impossible to evacuate Sears, he had everyone get under the main beam, which turned out to be a good decision, for it held firmly. He related how frightening it was as the windows shattered, the small appliances jumped off the shelves, the

216

movements of large appliances threatened them from all directions, and a large fissure opened where they were standing. Fortunately, no one was hurt, but two of his employees were so badly shaken that they left Alaska for therapy.

Next, Glenn became our main concern. He had a camera concession at Penney's and his main store was only a block north. We hoped that the delay was because he was trying to secure the building because of all the expensive photographic merchandise. Little did we know that his car was standing on its nose in the same hole into which his store had slumped. A friend brought him home and he told how he had stood in the middle of 4th Avenue and watched his building and those in the next block drop the equivalent of one floor.

With each account the incredible story of the destruction grew, but it was many hours later before we learned of the disaster in Turnagain, Anchorage's most exclusive residential neighborhood. Seventy-seven homes were destroyed.

Turnagain area home

Sixty-five others had to be evacuated, and 360 homes showed varying amounts of damage. The new bluff line is now several blocks inland from where it was before the quake.

That night we stayed with our good friends, Dorothy and John Toney (our neighbors to the south.) There was no power, thus no heat. Again, we were thankful for our fireplaces. Even more important was the warmth of being with our best friends—our neighbors. We had two transistors and alternated between Anchorage Civil Defense and a Fairbanks radio station. Things looked pretty glum here, and then we heard about Valdez, then Kodiak, and, oh no, Seward too! How isolated we felt! All communications cut, bridges collapsed, roads wrecked, docks demolished, and airport runways inoperable. How were our other friends? Were they alive? Did they even have a place to stay? How long would the food last?

Civil Defense advised us to back our cars out of our garages into our driveways and be ready to spend the night in them in case we should get another high intensity quake and have to evacuate our houses.

"A tidal wave is heading for Anchorage!" was the urgent radio message. "All people in the Bootlegger's Cove and Turnagain area, evacuate immediately." Haven't those poor people had enough? Tensely we waited it out. "It should reach Anchorage by 11 pm." By 11:30 pm we began to relax. Somehow we had been spared.

Wednesday night, April 8:

There are so many of your questions to answer, but finding the time is the real problem. Students returned to Wendler Junior High today. We teachers had been working there several days earlier.

Even now, twelve days later, we are still stunned. We find a great deal of comfort in visiting, comparing notes on experiences, or relating those of others. "How did you make out?" and, "Did you hear about...," are earthquake clichés.

Today in all of my classes students talked about their experiences. It would have been futile to have tried anything else, for they needed the therapy of sharing it. Tomorrow we go back to modern math and science. I've made a seismograph to record aftershocks and prepared units on earthquakes, tsunamis (improperly called tidal waves) and typhoid.

West High School students are on double shift at East, our other high school. Romig, the new junior high school to which I was to transfer next year, will probably house West High students next year. Government Hill School, which dropped down the hill, and Denali, which was just con-

Government Hill School

demned, are double shifting with two other elementary schools.

Anchorage Community College, which met at night at West High, is now in scattered locations. Alaska Methodist University, Alaska Psychiatric Clinic, and Providence Hospital are all within one mile of Wendler Junior High. Their buildings, like ours, are in fair shape.

Two more elementary schools will reopen tomorrow. Another school can't open until other housing is found for the 300 homeless Alaskan Native people who were evacuated to Anchorage when their villages were wiped out by the tsunami.

NBC News at Sears

Connie talked with the city manager and Lease Company, which has the contract for the demolition of Penney's, again today. They are to erect a retaining wall to keep on the north side of the street. Connie hopes to be able to reopen Sears, which is just down the street on the north side, on Monday. He expects it to be slow for a while.

With proper identification, store managers and owners were the only ones besides the rescue and work crews allowed in the badly damaged downtown area. Of course, Connie always had his camera with him. One day he was taking some pictures in front of the Sears store and another fellow with cameras asked him what outfit he was with. When Connie pointed to Sears, he seemed surprised. Connie returned the question. The fellow with all the cameras was representing the Saturday Evening Post. NBC's newsman, Joe Rich, from Tokyo, took movies from a spot in front of Sears. It was a good angle to shoot pictures of the damage to Penney's.

All of the major magazines have been here. Connie has taken some excellent pictures, and so many people want copies. He could have sold them many times if he had wanted to, but after working hard all day trying to get

Robert Atwood's home

things back in order, he doesn't feel like working four or five more hours every night in the darkroom. At present there is not a place left which develops pictures commercially. Connie has, however, given sets to many of the Sears and Allstate people who have been up and say they need them.

One night Civil Defense Headquarters called and asked if he would develop some pictures for Governor Egan to take to Washington, D.C. the next morning. Unfortunately, we don't have to equipment to develop the 20-inch pictures that he needed.

Last Friday, just one week after the big shock, we had another strong aftershock (6.5 on the Richter Scale). Connie and Glenn McLain both claim they set new records for the 50 yard dash. Connie and one of his salesmen actually hurdled the high sales counter on their way out. They didn't want to get trapped in that building again.

After what people went through, it is no wonder that some needed to be sent outside (of Alaska), for therapy.

Leora Knight, a teacher friend of mine, died a terrible death trying to get out of their home on the bluff. Her body was torn by the opposite sides of a separated sidewalk. Her husband was holding her hand and his leg was cut off. He is still in the hospital and they may have to amputate his other leg.

Bill Taylor, who was killed when the control tower at Anchorage International Airport collapsed, was the father of one of my former students. Connie and I used to visit him sometimes when he was on duty. He said they liked the company.

The situation in Turnagain is almost beyond comprehension. Blocks and blocks of once beautiful homes rode, split, crumbled, fell, or balanced precariously as the shift-

Four Seasons Apartments

ing, sifting sand sloughed off. As Dr. Mead's house became a victim, it, in turn, claimed two of his children. Dr. Martin lost a $90,000 home; however, it is his comment which lingers with me. "I was very lucky. All I lost was a house."

Robert Atwood, publisher of Alaska's largest newspaper and owner of one of the nicest homes in Turnagain, wrote of his battle for survival. As the fissures developed, he fell into one and was almost buried by the sand. Once out he tried to climb a fence and the fence disappeared under him. He saw his neighbor's house disappear. Trees and mailboxes slid away.

One family of four couldn't get out. They huddled in the hallway. The floor rose under them. Soon they would be crushed against the ceiling. Suddenly the roof split and they were lifted free and safe.

A couple of geologists told me that the reason it was so bad in Turnagain was that when the quake started, the clay, which is under the gravel and sand, acted like lubricating fluid. We don't have permafrost around here, but the ground was frozen to about five feet deep this year. If this quake had occurred after the thaw, it would have been much worse, for instead of fissuring and going down on blocks of frozen ground, each subsequent row of houses would have buried the houses and people who were in the part that had sloughed off before them.

Our friends, Ruth and Glenn McLain, lost two business locations, their main store, the Camera center, and the concession that they had in the Penney's store. They have finally found a small place where they can relocate. They lost a great deal by damage to delicate equipment and by looting at Penney's. The man from National Cash Register told Connie that someone of "professional" caliber had emptied all the registers at Penney's. Fortunately, Connie had the foresight to lug that heavy cash register to the car and brought it home with him. Fortunately, the looting that was done was minor. What was done probably occurred Friday night before the Alaska National Guard was on patrol and keeping everyone out but the rescue teams.

The Federal Building is in good shape, for it has large expansion joints and meets specifications of a San Francisco Post Office, but that was not true of many other buildings. Fifty construction workers had worked on the six story Four Season Apartment Building minutes before it was reduced to a pile of rubble.

There were four or five tense days after gas escaped into Cook Inlet. They estimated that a million gallons of jet fuel also escaped at Anchorage International Airport, which is only a block from our house. No fire of any kind was al-

Hillside Apartments

lowed anywhere near the water or the airport. We weren't just lucky not to have any fires. It was due to the careful planning of officials and the great cooperation of people in the community.

We have many things to be thankful for. We didn't have a serious fire. The predicted "tidal wave" didn't occur—probably for a couple reasons. It was low tide and the momentum of the water would have been dissipated by glancing from one side of the Cook Inlet to the other. The timing of the quake at the end of winter and not at the beginning, for there was plenty of snow for fresh drinking water. It was a school holiday, so most families were together. People were on the way home or had just arrived so they didn't have time to light a fire in the fireplace. The Anchorage Port is operable and the damage is covered by insurance. It's the only one left in this large area of Alaska. There has not been even one case of typhoid. The Alaska National Guard was in encampment near here and they and the people from the two military bases helped us in so many vital ways.

Now the worst is over, we can look back and laugh at many things. During the quake a drunk staggered out a downtown bar and finally grabbed a parking meter for support. As he was clinging to it, everything sank the equivalent of one floor. Not aware of what was really happening, the drunk calmly staggered off as if he were merely leaving an elevator.

Mac's Foto Store

An emloyee at Chrysler was so frightened that he dashed outside, jumped into the car and drove off. Two days later he discovered that it wasn't his car.

An attorney wanted his files so much that he entered the Hillside Apartments which had been declared unsafe and tiptoed ever so quietly so no one would discover him inside. A woman in the street yelled, "There she goes!" Thinking she meant the building, he jumped out the second floor window and broke his ankle.

Mac's Foto Store crumpled into a deep hole. A new sign appeared. "Due to early breakup, moved to 7th and C." Another business that has a two foot fissure running under it has this sign. "We know it's hard to make a living, but we didn't expect to go in the hole!"

Earl Hillstrand and Governor Egan flew to Homer to survey the damage there. The Homer Spit has sunk approximately six feet, and Earl's lodge, Land's End, at the tip of the spit, now has water up to the bar stools at high tide, but he still has his sense of humor. When Governor Egan asked Earl what he was going to do, he replied, "Guess I'll have to raise the bar stools."

After we heard that a mile of Seward's waterfront had slid into Resurrection Bay, we were concerned about the safety of our friends who live near the Seward Small Boat Harbor, for we had also heard that when the tsunami hit the Seward Harbor, it threw all the boats ashore and made kindling out of most of them. We had accepted the idea that our boat was part of that kindling pile, but when Doug called to

Locomotive

say that they were all right, he had surprising news for us.
We had been working on our boat (again and again) and it
was parked on its clunker of a trailer by the harbormaster's
two story cement block house. The tsunami waves demolished the house apart and lifted our boat on its trailer
and dropped it and two railroad cars in Dottie and Doug's
front yard! Only two other boats besides ours survived the
tsunami in Seward.

On the road to Seward

We were also very concerned about Dr. Starr, for he had
gone fishing that day. Connie felt sure that he was out in
Thumb's Cove. We found out that he was and his experience is the marine parallel of Bob Atwood's story of survival. Dr. Starr was on the shore skinning a seal. His fishing
buddy was in the boat. The tsunami arrived unexpectedly.
Dr. Starr started running. Thinking he would only find a

floating body, his buddy searched the water. Then he heard a shout from high in a tree. Dr. Starr was safe. His friend moved in after him. The wave receded leaving them in the trees high and dry. Another wave came in and they rode it out in the trees.

We plan to drive to Seward and check on our boat as soon as the bridges are rebuilt. Many parts of the road are barely one-way now.

Still a bit shaken, but thankful for many things— especially for our good friends and neighbors. We're still glad that we live in Alaska.

Cordially,

Connie, Daisy Lee & Tim Bitter

Patty Jones Williams
Marching With The National Guard

WHEN THE "BIG ONE" HIT ALASKA, Richard, Ken and I were in Anchorage. Richard was doing his final inspection march in National Guard encampment. He was supposed to be finished after that.

Ken, our older son, then 2½, and I were staying a couple of days with Clara (Nielson) Gebhart and her boys who lived a little ways out of Anchorage. Clara and I went to school in Homer and were close friends. Gary, our other son, was 2 months old and with some people in Homer.

The boys were playing and we gals were visiting when the house started to shake. The house, being an old one, started swaying; it had lots of give. Clara and I decided we didn't want to be trapped in the house if it collapsed, so the only other choice was to get outside. As soon as we got through the small entry porch and stepped onto the ground we found it was impossible to stand up. We sat down in the snow with the boys in our laps and watched the trees, houses, land and power poles swaying and rolling. After the worse part was over and we decided we could walk, we looked up and realized we were sitting under power lines. The house seemed like a lot safer place, so we went back inside.

Richard said when he was marching it felt like he was getting dizzy from moving ground, then everyone realized it was an earthquake. The power lines **The power lines started snapping and cracking—and fire was flying** started snapping and cracking—and fire was flying.

In the distance was a hill that looked like ocean swells the way it was rolling. When he looked back at the bank, the tuba player was lying on the ground. He glanced toward the barracks and our car was sliding about 40 feet back and forth.

After the troops were sent back to the barracks, they were told it was a statewide emergency and they would not be released as planned. Richard and his group were sent to the International Airport armory to aid the homeless by giving out water and furnishing shelter there.

Ken and I flew back to Homer as Richard would be there for some time with our car and we were worried if there was any damage to our house. Because the Sterling Highway was closed, we had to have the car shipped to us in a flying-boxcar plane.

Patty (Burton) Shroy
Refugees In Our Own Home

GOOD FRIDAY! That day has different meanings for different people, but to me and five of my brothers and sisters, it meant a day of no school, a day to hang out in our pajamas and watch TV. My Mom and Aunt were at J.C. Penney's shopping for Easter. Dad was a few miles away rebuilding our family home that had burned to the ground the previous summer. Our new home was still on the east side of town, at the foot of the Chugach Mountains.

We were in our particular kind of heaven, just finished watching the cartoon "Johnny Quest" and anxiously awaiting "Fireball XL-5." I was ten years old at the time; the oldest there was my brother Jim at fourteen, and the youngest was my sister Kathy, who had just turned two. A light snow was falling outside, and we were scattered leisurely around the living room when the TV went out. We looked at each other in shocked dismay, "Fireball XL-5" had just begun and we were going to miss it! That was something we could make sense of and that had some point of reference. What happened immediately after that was something we didn't understand.

The house began to shake, HARD. There was a rumbling that seemed to come from everywhere at once. The cupboards in the kitchen began to fly open, dishes spilling out onto the floor. The house, that before had seemed so sturdy and safe, was now creaking and moaning, moving around in ways that didn't seem possible. It was my brother Jim that finally made the connection, "EARTHQUAKE! Everybody get out of the house!" We ran out the door, everyone oblivious to the snowy ground and the cold, still in our nightclothes and bare feet. The frozen ground was ROLLING like waves, trees were jiggling and swaying madly in all directions. There was nowhere we could stand that would get us away from this immense power that surrounded us.

We stood there for what seemed like minutes. In fact, time seemed to stretch on through the whole experience. Every moment was expanded. Then someone yelled, "Kathy is still in the house!" Jim ran in to get her. He found her wide-eyed, sitting on the couch that was rolling from one end of the living room to the other. He brought her out, then directed us to the car, "Put your foot on the brake," and ran back in for blankets. We had done all we could do and the earthquake was still in full force. I was more frightened than I had ever been, but as I was sitting there with both feet pressed hard on the brake, it came to me that there exists in life events in which we have no control. In that moment I experienced acceptance and an inner calm and it is a moment that I will never forget.

We found out later that my Mom and Aunt had left J.C. Penney's just prior to the collapse of a brick wall. A classmate of Mom's had been killed there. Mom was driving home and at first couldn't make sense of the trees whipping around and why the car had no forward motion when she stepped on the gas. My Dad had been knocked off the roof and was hanging onto the eave, geysers from broken pipes erupting all around.

We spent the next several days camped in our living room along with my Grandfather, my Aunt and Uncle and our seven cousins. It felt safe to be with family. We had no power, heat or water. The bedrooms were on the upper and lower levels of the house. We all opted to stay on the ground floor. The bathroom was on the upper level, and I remember running up there and back in the fastest possible time. There were countless aftershocks during that time, so our caution was not unwarranted. None of them were as strong as the first, but we feared the possibilities. It took a long time to get information about the rest of the city and the state. It was an uncertain time. Our security had been shaken, we had become refugees in our own home.

Benjamin B. Talley
The Rehabilitation Of Anchorage

FROM 1941 TO 1943 I had been the U.S. Army Corps of Engineers Officer in Charge of Construction for the tremendous program of building the bases (including Elmendorf, Adak, Amchitka, Shemya and others on the mainland and in the Aleutians, along with numerous airfields, ports, the Whittier Tunnels, and other projects.) I retired from the Army in 1956, and in 1964 I returned to Alaska to be in charge of the engineering for the rehabilitation of the greater Anchorage area after the devastating Good Friday earthquake of 1964. That was my first contact with the Corps of Engineers as a civilian.

When the earthquake occurred and Anchorage suffered as much as it did, the area was declared a disaster area. The people of Anchorage went to the District Engineer and asked the District Engineer to take action through the Corps. The District Engineer was Colonel Kenneth T. Sawyer.

When the people of Anchorage called on the Corps, the Corps then called Metcalf and Eddy of Boston to ask them to consider negotiating for handling the engineering. The sudden load imposed upon the District was more than they could handle without a great influx of personnel—of perhaps 25 additional highly-skilled engineers. So as the Corps does in cases like that, they select an architect-engineering firm to do the in-house engineering. They selected Metcalf and Eddy.

Metcalf and Eddy Engineers was a partnership. Andy Patton, one of the top people in the firm, telephoned Joe

Benjamin B. Talley

Markle, a lawyer in New York who specialized in construction matters, and asked, "Can you name somebody that we could pick to be charge of the work in Alaska?" Joe knew of my earlier work in Alaska. He called me on the telephone in Oklahoma where I was operating a ranch. Joe asked me if I was interested in going to Alaska. I told him, "Yes." We had a conference telephone call between his office in New York, Metcalf & Eddy in Boston and myself, and we decided right then that I would go. That was on the Thursday following the Good Friday earthquake. On Sunday, I was in New York. On Monday, I was in Boston, and on Tuesday morning about 8:30 I was in Anchorage.

I checked into a motel in Anchorage and had scarcely had time to unpack when I was asked to attend a conference concerning the water and sewer systems in the city. City representatives declared that the entire water and sewer systems needed replacement. I expressed surprise, since at the downtown motel where I was staying, I had water coming from the tap, and I was able to flush the toilet. In the course of the next several months we developed a kind of flat, motorized cart on which a man could go through the sewers to determine whether damage had occurred.

We worked well with the Corps District office just as though we were a part of that office. Our position was the same as that of an engineer in the District office. He doesn't make the decision for the client. He may tell the client what he will recommend to the District Engineer, but it is the District Engineer who makes the final decision. We were doing the engineering. Anchorage representatives came to us with problems, particularly to determine whether or not it was proper for the federal government, through the Corps of Engineers, to pay for the cost of the rehabilitation of an item or whether it was not. That was the big question.

The Rehabilitation Of Anchorage

In the course of our engineering work following the earthquake, which continued throughout 1964, we found a number of unusual situations. For example, there was a house which had been unoccupied for a lengthy period. In the kitchen, the refrigerator had slid across the dusty floor in a zigzag manner. Its trail in the dust showed the direction and strength of each of the numerous shocks. Marks on the walls to which pictures were attached also showed the direction and strength of the various shock waves.

There were two identical buildings in downtown Anchorage located a few blocks apart but sited in different directions. One was damaged substantially; the other escaped almost unharmed. One of the engineers in my office determined by mathematical calculations that neither would have been damaged substantially if the height had been reduced by one story.

The force of the earthquake squeezed the water from a stratum of blue clay which underlies part of the area. This caused a number of buildings to slide. Some disappeared into Cook Inlet. In at least one instance, a large apartment building slid several feet but except for broken water, electric and sewer lines, was relatively unscathed. It came to rest on real estate which did not belong to the apartment owners. Situations such as this raised legal questions of ownership. After the earthquake it was necessary for surveyors to establish new base lines and to refigure the location and ownership of numerous properties. When one drives up L Street in downtown Anchorage, at about 9th Avenue you can notice a distinct setback of the street curb which resulted from the earth movement.

The U.S. Geological Survey studied the earthquake area and found that certain parts of Anchorage are potentially unstable and are therefore particularly subject to earthquake damage. Any high rise buildings in those areas are especially at risk.

Because I was a former officer of the Corps, I could not handle any negotiations at all with the Corps of Engineers. For example, when the time came for an extension of the contract and an enlargement of it, I could have no part in that negotiation. I attended the conferences with Mr. Patton, Vice President of Metcalf and Eddy, who came to Alaska to handle the negotiations. I was just listed as one of those present.

Quite a number of the engineers who came out from Boston had been on active duty with the Corps of Engineers during the war. So I would say, within a couple of weeks the position of the engineers in my office was very little different from that of the other engineers in the District.

We had a Corps engineer liaison officer in our office in our engineering division. He kept abreast of what we were doing. I would take up the touchy subjects with him. Thus, I knew what the Corps wanted, and I also made sure that I was doing what the Corps wanted. Insofar as I know, our recommendations were all accepted by the District Engineer. There was never one that was not, because we worked together.

We had two cases which caused some controversy. The Highway Department of the State of Alaska had a yard—shops and office, storage yard, equipment repair shop and that sort of thing—in downtown Anchorage. A couple of the buildings were damaged. The Anchorage representatives came to me and said, "We want you to declare those buildings a total loss, and we want to be reimbursed for that damage. We want to build a new yard out of town. We want to get rid of this one, so we want you to back us up here and say that those buildings cannot be economically rehabilitated and therefore should be torn down." I said, "I can't do it. I won't recommend that to the Corps. If you want to, you talk to the Corps about it, but I think I can tell you right now what they'll tell you." The man came back to my office two or three times, and I stood my ground. Whether he ever went to the Corps, I don't know. Finally he said, "I'll be back next week, and maybe you'll change your mind by the time I get back." He went to Juneau and tried to put all the political pressure that he could possibly put on the Corps and on me as an individual to recommend to the Corps that those buildings be declared a total loss, and I wouldn't do it. He left in a big huff and more or less let me know, "Oh, you'll find out in the future about these things."

There was another case which was touchy. There is one section of the city where a firm of local engineers recommended that we replace every manhole in quite a large subdivision. The firm engineer came to me about it and wanted me to approve that recommendation. I hadn't been out there, because it hadn't been my job to go out and look at those things. I sent for our engineer who was responsible for that area and asked his opinion. He said, "No, those shouldn't be replaced. Some of these manholes are more than two feet in diameter and are ten or fifteen feet deep. No more than two or three of them out of more than 100 are broken up."

Although the local engineer recommended to us that they all be replaced, I said, "I can't recommend that to the Corps." He and I got into quite a discussion. He went over my head and made the direct recommendation to the Corps that all the manholes in the major sewers of that entire subdivision be replaced. The Corps engineer called us out and wanted to know what we thought. We gave them the reasons. I didn't know what the engineer was going to recommend to the district engineer. I told him "It is our considered opinion and judgment that these need not be replaced, and if you do direct they be replaced, then I ask that we have nothing to do with the engineering, the design of it, because it's our professional opinion that they do not require replacement." They didn't replace them.

In only those two instances was there any serious conflict. In some instances, the city tried to get as much as it could from the federal government, and that's par for the course in any dealing with a political entity. I had good rapport with the District Engineer. Perhaps half a dozen people in the District office in 1964 were there when I left in 1943. It's a little unusual to go back under contract to your old office that you opened, some 20 years after you left. We had a very, very happy relationship there. By the end of 1964, my wife and I had decided that we wanted to live in Alaska, and it was at that time that we purchased the property on which I am now living in Anchor Point.

Alaska Earthquake 1964
Where were you?

ARE YOU READY FOR THE NEXT ONE?

Sandy McDaniel
On Being Prepared

THE EXPERIENCES AND RECOLLECTIONS of Alaskans who survived the Good Friday quake in 1964 are dramatic, awe inspiring, difficult even to imagine.[†] This historical data on earthquakes in Alaska is equally dramatic. Originally reported at a magnitude of 8.4 on the Richter scale, scientists have revised figures for the '64 quake to 9.2. In the last hundred years three of the ten largest earthquakes world wide have happened in Alaska (see the chart on page 265). During that same time span thirty-five quakes of magnitude 7.2 or higher have occurred on the Kenai Peninsula.

Perhaps most important to those of us currently living in this magnificent, trembling state, the historical pattern for the occurrence of major earthquakes in Alaska is once every fifteen years. We are now in the thirtieth year since a major quake, fifteen years overdue according to the established pattern. Inspires one to pause in the midst of the daily routine, doesn't it?

Perhaps you could extend that pause to include a few minutes each day to make a plan and gather a few supplies to prepare yourself, your home, and your work place for the possibility of an earthquake.

Alaskans are, generally speaking, independent, self sufficient people. Those qualities will stand us in good stead in

---

[†] Sandy McDaniel is a graduate of the Federal Energy Management Administration (FEMA) Earthquake Safety program.

Sandy McDaniel

times of emergency. We are also physically isolated. That is
the nature of our state. In 1964 the first loads of relief supplies were not gathered and on the way to Alaska until
forty-eight hours later.

Having a plan and some supplies in place would certainly make the first three to five days after an earthquake
easier to survive, easier on the survivors.

Please, take a few moments to read through the following recommendations. Then act on them. Anything you do
now will benefit you, your loved ones, and your community.

©1994 Sandy McDaniel

F.E.M.A.
Are You Ready?

EARTHQUAKES

A N EARTHQUAKE IS a sudden shaking of the earth caused by breaking and shifting of rock beneath the earth's surface. Earthquakes can cause buildings and bridges to collapse, down telephone and power lines and result in fires, explosions and landslides. Earthquakes can also cause huge ocean waves, called tsunamis, which travel long distances over water until they crash into coastal areas.

Earthquake injuries are usually caused by building collapse or windows, overturned furniture, and fires from broken chimneys and ruptured gas and electrical lines. Injuries may also be caused by collapsing bridges and elevated roadways.

Scientists can't precisely predict when earthquakes will occur. Populations in forty-one states or territories are at moderate to high risk. Earthquakes occur most often in states west of the Rocky Mountains, but violent earthquakes have also occurred in the eastern U.S. All states are at some risk from this hazard.

EARTHQUAKE PREPAREDNESS STEPS

1. Check for hazards that could make your house more dangerous during an earthquake:
   - Repair defective electrical wiring, leaky gas and inflexible utility connections. Bolt down water heaters and gas appliances.
   - Know where and how to shut off electricity, gas and water at main switches and valves. Check with your local utilities for instructions.
   - Place large or heavy objects on lower shelves. Securely fasten shelves to walls. Brace or anchor high or top-heavy objects.
   - Store bottled foods, glass, china and other breakables on low shelves or cabinets that can be fastened shut.
   - Anchor overhead lighting fixtures solidly in place.
   - Check and repair deep plaster cracks in ceilings and foundations. Get expert advice, especially if there are signs of structural defects.
2. Be sure the house is firmly anchored to its foundations.
3. Hold occasional earthquake drills so each member of your family knows what to do during an earthquake.
4. Locate safe spots in each room—under sturdy tables or desks or in strong, supported doorways. Reinforce this information by physically placing yourself and your family in these locations.
5. Identify danger zones in each room—near windows where glass can shatter or near bookcases or other furniture that may fall over. During an earthquake, each

family member should move away from these danger zones to the nearest safe spot.

6. Gather emergency supplies and prepare for evacuation if earthquake damage is severe.
7. Develop a family plan for reuniting after an earthquake. Establish an out-of state telephone contact and leave notes for other family members if you must relocate.
8. Review insurance to determine coverage for earthquake damage. Some damage may be covered even without specific earthquake insurance. Protect important home and business papers.

WHAT TO DO DURING AN EARTHQUAKE

1. Keep calm, and stay where you are. Most injuries during an earthquake occur when people decide to enter or exit buildings.
2. If you are indoors, take cover under a desk, table or bench, against an inside wall or solid heavy framed doorway, and hold on. Stay away from glass, windows, outside doors or walls and anything that could fall and hurt you, such as lighting, furniture or fixtures.
3. If you are outdoors, stay there. Move away from buildings, street lights and utility wires.
4. If you are in a crowded public place, do not rush for a doorway—other people will have the same idea. Take cover, and move away from display shelves containing objects that may fall.
5. In a high-rise building, get under a desk, away from windows and outside walls. Stay in the building on the same floor. Do not be surprised if the electricity goes out or if sprinkler systems or elevator or fire alarms go on—this often happens. Do not use elevators!

6. If you are in a moving vehicle, stop as quickly as safety permits, and stay in the vehicle. Avoid stopping near or under buildings, trees, overpasses or utility wires. Then proceed cautiously, watching for road and bridge damage.

WHAT TO DO AFTER AN EARTHQUAKE

1. Be prepared for aftershocks, which occur from less than one minute after the initial shock to more than one year later. These secondary shock-waves are usually less violent than the main quake but can be strong enough to do additional damage to weakened structures.
2. Check for injuries. Do not attempt to move seriously injured persons unless they are in immediate danger of death or further injury.
   - If you must move an unconscious person, first stabilize the neck and back, then call for help immediately.
   - If the victim is not breathing but has good pupil reflex, carefully position the victim for artificial resuscitation.
   - Maintain body temperature with blankets. Be sure the victim does not become overheated.
   - Never try to feed liquids to an unconscious person.
3. Stay out of severely damaged buildings. Return to your home when authorities say it is safe to do so.
4. Use flashlights or battery powered lanterns. Do not use candles, matches or open flames indoors after the earthquake because of possible gas leaks.
5. Wear sturdy shoes in areas covered with fallen debris and broken glass.

6. Clean up spilled medicines, bleaches, gasoline and other flammable liquids inside buildings. Evacuate the building if gasoline fumes are heavy and the building is not well ventilated.
7. Visually inspect utility lines, chimneys and appliances for damage.
    - If you smell gas, open windows and shut off the main gas valve. Leave the building immediately and report the leak to the gas company. Stay out of the building until no gas odor remains.
    - If you see electrical damage, switch off all electrical power at the main box.
    - If you can see that water pipes are damaged, shut off water supply at the main valve.
    - Do not switch on gas or electricity until the utility company has checked your home.
    - Do not flush toilets until you know that sewage lines are intact.
    - Check chimneys for cracks and damage. The initial check should be made from a distance. Approach chimneys with great cautions. Have a professional inspect the chimney for internal damage before lighting a fire.
    - If water is cut off, use water from water heaters.
    - Open doors cautiously. Beware of objects that may tumble off shelves.
    - Use the phone only to report a life threatening emergency.
8. Turn on your battery-operated radio (or plug in your radio or television if you still have electricity) to get the latest emergency information.
9. Stay off the streets. If you must go out, travel with care. Watch for hazards created by the earthquake, such as

fallen objects, downed electrical wires, weakened bridges, roads and sidewalks.

10. Stay away from damaged areas unless your assistance has been specifically requested by police, fire or relief organizations.

11. If you live near coastal waters, be aware of possible tsunamis, also known as tidal waves. When local authorities issue a tsunami warning, assume that a series of dangerous waves is on the way. Stay away from the beach.

TSUNAMIS

A TSUNAMI,[†] SOMETIMES CALLED A TIDAL WAVE, is actually a series of enormous waves created by an underwater disturbance or earthquake. Tsunamis can move hundreds of miles per hour in the open ocean and smash into land with waves more than 100 feet high. In this century, more than 200 tsunamis have been recorded in the Pacific Ocean alone.

All tsunamis are potentially dangerous, even though they many not damage every coastline they strike—some waves in the series are less hazardous than others.

Tsunamis can strike anywhere along most of the U.S. coastline. The most destructive tsunamis have occurred along the coasts of California, Oregon, Washington, Alaska and Hawaii.

HOW TO PREPARE FOR A TSUNAMI

1. Heed tsunami warnings—they mean a tsunami exists. Listen to radio or television for information and follow instructions of your local authorities.

[†] Pronounced soo–nahm–ee

2. Advance warning of tsunamis sometimes comes in the form of a noticeable rise or fall in the normal depth of coastal water. This is nature's tsunami warning and should be heeded.
3. If you feel an earthquake in a Pacific coast area, turn on your battery powered radio to learn if there is a tsunami warning.
4. A small tsunami at one beach can be a giant wave a few miles away. Do not let the modest size of one wave allow you to forget how dangerous tsunamis are. The next wave may be bigger.
5. Prepare ahead for possible evacuation.

WHAT TO DO IF A TSUNAMI THREATENS

1. If you are advised to evacuate, do so immediately.
2. Stay away from the area until local authorities say it is safe. Do not be fooled into thinking that the danger is over when a single wave has come and gone—a tsunami is not a single wave but a series of waves.
3. Do not go to the shoreline to watch for a tsunami. When you can see the wave, it is too late to escape it.

Susan Price
Welcome to Earthquake Country

W ELCOME TO EARTHQUAKE COUNTRY. It's only a matter of time.[†] The Los Angeles quake on January 17 measured a 6.7 magnitude on the moment-magnitude scale and 6.8 on the surface-wave magnitude scale. In contrast, Alaska averages 4½ earthquakes at magnitude 6 or greater each year, according to Peter Haeussler, a U.S. Geological Survey geologist.

Seven of the 10 largest earthquakes ever recorded in the United States occurred in Alaska. Three of the world's 10 largest earthquakes in history occurred in Alaska. So far this century, Alaska has averaged a magnitude 8.0 earthquake or larger every 13 years and the state hasn't had one that big since 1965.

As for Homer, it falls into the Cook Inlet area, which is one of the two most active earthquake areas in the state, Haeussler said. Even the na-

Homer ... is one of the two most active earthquake areas in the state

tional Uniform Building Code classifies Cook Inlet as its most dangerous earthquake zone, said Paul Whitmore, a geophysicist with the Tsunami Warning Center in Palmer.

The Cook Inlet area is active because two tectonic plates, the Pacific and North American, rub against each other. "Homer is lying on top of where this happens,"

[†] Susan Price was a staff reporter for The Homer News.
This article appeared in the Feb 17, 1994 issue.

Haeussler said. "Plates stick together for a bit, unstick and slip. When they slip, that causes an earthquake. The odds of an earthquake are virtually 100 percent, even of something big. It's just a matter of time when something big will happen."

That's just the point the Homer Volunteer Fire Department and others are trying to bring home. It's only a matter of time before an earthquake, possibly accompanied by a tsunami, hits Homer—so it's critical that people start thinking about what they'll do now.

To help, the Homer fire department is holding a free earthquake class Thursday of next week at 6:30 pm at Homer City Hall. Panel speakers will include Whitmore and Bob Heavilin, the Kenai Peninsula Borough's emergency management coordinator; Homer Fire Chief Robert Purcell and Mike Daugherty, who's Homer's police chief and is head of the city's Department of Public Safety. Pinkston Enterprise's Bill Morse, a consultant who put together the borough's disaster plan, will also speak.

The class will outline what people can expect from local agencies, but more importantly, what they'll have to do for themselves. "There's an unrealistic expectation on the part of the public that help (will be) just a phone call away," Purcell said. "In a major earthquake or tsunami, those resources won't be available."

Homer area's handful of volunteers—roughly 35 firefighters and 35 medics—won't go far if, in the worst case scenario, 300 to 400 people are injured, the only road in is blocked and the airport can't be used, Purcell said. Outside help could be 24 hours or longer away, particularly if the quake hits other parts of Alaska too.

"A lot of things people need to do for themselves. That's what we want to teach people," Purcell said. Much of what people can do to their homes or businesses before an earthquake is basic, and cheap. Some of it's just being organized by setting aside survival items and those that might be needed in an evacuation. A lot is knowing what to do, say, to shut off a propane gas or fuel-oil tank valve. "This community only has a couple days' food on the shelves in the store. And a great deal of it will be destroyed," Purcell said. The experts say it pays to be ready ahead of time. Heavilin and Purcell listed some ideas:

- Heavilin has three buzz words to describe what to do: *duck, cover and hold.* If you're in bed, Heavilin said to stay there and cover yourself with blankets and pillows. If you're inside, get under a desk or table and cover your neck and head. Or stand in a doorway bracing yourself. If that's not possible, sit against an inside wall. If you're outside, get out in the open, away from buildings, trees and powerlines, and sit down. If you're driving, stop the car away from buildings or bridges, but stay in the car, Heavilin said. As the Tsunami Warning Center's Whitmore said, "the ground-shaking itself won't kill anybody, but the collapse of a building or bridge will."

- At home, fix what Heavilin calls the "nonstructural hazards"—those things inside homes, businesses and schools that are heavy and will fall over if the ground starts to shake. Heavy things that fall injure people as well as block exits. Freestanding bookshelves or filing cabinets can spell trouble. For example, Purcell described how a man was sleeping just before the Los Angeles earthquake, but had gotten up for a quick snack when the quake hit. He walked back to his bedroom to find a huge shelving unit that had fallen on his bed.

257

- Move things that could tip over or break away from beds, such as big picture frames, shelving, hanging light fixtures or televisions up high. Beds should be kept away from big windows and heavy objects should be stored on lower shelves.
- Bolt down or fasten items to keep them from shifting..

For example, Heavilin said he's attached eye screws to a wall in his living room and connected a wire from the wall to the back of heavy items such a stereo speakers. He said he collects toothpick holders and has them on a ledge in his living room. To keep them from crashing to the floor, he's run an invisible railing of fishing line across the front of the ledge. In his kitchen, Heavilin said he has installed conventional child-proof latches on each cabinet to keep the cabinet's contents from falling out onto the floor. Purcell said a 1-inch by 2-inch piece of wood can be screwed onto pantry shelves. That could keep food in glass jars intact as well as protect antique dishes or family heirlooms. "It might make a difference between saving your stuff and having a pile of glass on the floor," Heavilin said.

Susan Price
Earthquake Class

N O ONE KNOWS WHEN THE BIG QUAKE WILL HIT Alaska and Homer but the experts agree that it's inevitable.[†] And they all agree that preparation now will more than pay for itself. The message is clear. "Given the approximately 45 volunteer firefighters and medics in Homer, help will be spread thin, particularly for the first 24 to 48 hours after an earthquake or tsunami," said Homer Fire Chief Robert Purcell.

Purcell said people will have to know how to fend for themselves. A lot of that hinges on getting ready ahead of time. That's why the Homer Volunteer Fire Department has organized a free earthquake class tonight at 6:30 at Homer City Hall. WKFL cable television will broadcast the meeting live on Channel 3. The class' five speakers will outline things people can do to prepare for a disaster, what to do once it hits, and what type of help people can expect from local agencies.

No one knows when the Big Quake will hit Alaska and Homer but the experts agree that it's inevitable.

Last week's Homer News included a list of ideas of what people can do to get ready for the big quake and many of the ideas are easy and inexpensive. Purcell and Bob Heav-

---

[†]This article originally appeared in the Feb 24, 1994 issue of the Homer News.

ilin, the Kenai Peninsula Borough's emergency management coordinator, have more ideas:

Set aside survival items in a closet or garage that could be used after an earthquake or other emergency. Some of those items can go in a backpack or duffel bag, which would serve as a ready evacuation bag. Enough water and canned food, food bars and dehydrated food should be set aside to last at least three days but optimally two weeks.

Other items to set aside include an ABC-rated fire extinguisher, a radio that can operate on batteries, flashlights, spare batteries, a first-aid kit and first-aid handbook and sleeping bags or blankets. Plastic trash bags can also be helpful, along with work gloves, goggles to work around glass, duck tape, a crow bar and a filter mask such as those used for painting. Plastic sheeting can help with leaky roofs, and a fire-resistant strong box can keep birth certificates and even family pictures safe. Money, including change for pay phones, is a good idea. There's no guarantee bank automated-teller machines will be working, Heavilin said. Other useful items include prescription medicine, extra pairs of eye glasses and even baby wipes, he said.

The estimates vary, but Heavilin said two gallons of water should be set aside for each person per day. It's a good idea to keep liquid bleach and water purification tablets or drops such as iodine, Halazone or Globaline to disinfect water supplies. For a gallon of clear water, put in eight drops of bleach or 16 drops if it's cloudy. Let it stand 30 minutes, Heavilin said. Or, a 55-gallon drum can be filled half-way with water, then an ounce of bleach, then filled with water the rest of the way. Heavilin said people should never use dry or granulated bleach to disinfect water. Liquid bleach lasts about a year. Other water sources include the hot-water heater tanks, which hold 40 to 50 gallons and can be drained through a drain valve. The water in the back of toilets can also be used, Heavilin said.

Make sure everybody old enough in the house knows how to turn off fuse boxes—turn off individual breakers first, then main breakers—as well as fuel tank valves, the water main and propane-tank valves.

Hot-water heaters should be strapped to the wall so they won't topple over. Fuel tanks should be housed close to the ground on sturdy bolted-together cribs.

Propane bottles or tanks should be firmly anchored so they can't be knocked over. If they're next to a building, they should be hooked or chained to a wall. Purcell said it's also helpful to have a long connector hose to the bottle or tank that is partially flexible to allow for motion during an earthquake. Purcell said the three main fire causes after an earthquake include ones from natural or propane gas, electrical wires and heating systems such as woodstoves. Chimneys can fall apart, sending flames everywhere.

It's also a good idea to have some alternate heat source or a small generator. For instance, Purcell said he has an extra woodstove he can hook up if his electricity goes out.

Attach stereos, video-cassette recorders and computers to desks or tables with Velcro so they don't fly off onto the floor. One product, called "Quake Grip" has snaps plus the Velcro so things can be moved around when there's not a quake, Heavilin said.

Everyone in the house should carry in his or her wallet a card Heavilin calls an earthquake contact number. It's best if the number is the work and home number of someone who lives Outside. That way, if many of the Alaska phones are down and the family is separated, the family members can check in with each other through the Outside contact.

"It's all common sense stuff," Purcell said. And the work now might prove well worth the trouble, given a quake or any other disaster. Homer falls into the Cook Inlet area, which is one of the two most active earthquake areas in the state, said Peter Haeussler, a U.S. Geological Survey geologist.

The Cook Inlet area is active because two tectonic plates, the Pacific and North American, rub against each other. "Homer is lying on top of where this happens," Haeussler said. "The odds of an earthquake are virtually 100 percent," he said, "even of something big. It's just a matter of time when something big will happen."

Susan Price
Tsunami

EARTHQUAKES CAN FOSTER MEAN TSUNAMIS, and in Homer, some 1,000 people live or work in the area that would be caught if such a huge sea wave struck, an official said. A tsunami might even be worse than the earthquake that triggered it, according to Homer Fire Chief Robert Purcell, who is among public-safety officials sponsoring an earthquake-preparation class tonight. "The biggest threat to a large number of people is not so much an earthquake but the number 1 risk for a large life loss is a tsunami," he said.

Purcell said the worst-case scenario would be what seismologists call a 100-foot contour tsunami.[‡] In Homer, such a wave would cover everything up to Pioneer Avenue and East End Road, which is about the 100-foot elevation level, he said. Everyone in that area would have to be evacuated to higher ground.

The biggest threat to a large number of people is not so much an earthquake but ... a tsunami

But even with a more minor tsunami—one that would reach the 30- , 40- or 50-foot elevation—would drown the Spit, shoreline property and the Beluga Slough area, Purcell said. "A couple thousand people are on the Spit on a busy summer weekend," he said. "It would have to be self-evacuated—people in tents, hitchhikers, people fishing at

---

[‡] Some experts think the likelihood of a 100-foot contour tsunami in the Homer area is near zero. (Note added Feb 25, 1996).

the lagoon away from their vehicles. The frightening image we have is how that many people would get off the Spit successfully."

Paul Whitmore, a geophysicist with the Tsunami Warning Center in Palmer, said that only some earthquakes create tsunamis. But historically, in Alaska, they tend to.

Tsunamis usually only occur with earthquakes of a 7.0 magnitude or larger. They're created when there is a vertical uplift or down-drop in the sea floor that moves enough seawater to trigger a wave, Whitmore said. In contrast, the earthquakes in California tend to produce a horizontal motion along the fault and that won't generate a tsunami, he said.

Susan Price
The Ten Largest U.S. Earthquakes

EARTHQUAKES ARE MEASURED BY DIFFERENT SCALES: the surface-wave magnitude, the moment magnitude, the body-wave magnitude, the Richter and others, according to Bob Hammond, a geophysicist with the Alaska Earthquake Information Center in Palmer. The numerical value of the magnitude varies depending on the scale used to compute it.

	State	Date	Area	Surf. Wave/ Moment Mag.
1.	Alaska	Good Friday, 1964	Prince Wm. Sound	8.6 / 9.2
2.	Alaska	Sept. 10, 1899	Yakutat Bay	8.6 / na
3.	Alaska	Sept. 4, 1899	Yakutat Bay	8.3 / na
4.	Alaska	1900	Kodiak Island	8.3 / na
5.	Alaska	1903	Cape Providence	8.3 / na
6.	Alaska	1938	Shumagin Islands	8.3 / na
7.	Alaska	1957	Andreanof Islands	8.3[†] / 9.1
8.	California	1906	San Francisco	8.25/ na
9.	Missouri	1812	New Madrid	8.2 / na
10.	Missouri	1811	New Madrid	8.0 / na

The moment magnitude provides the most accurate measurement for earthquakes of magnitude 7.0 or larger but

---

[†] Based on body-wave scale. Sources: Alaska Earthquake Information Center, Palmer; National Earthquake Information Center, Denver.

265

moment magnitudes for numerous earthquakes in U.S. history haven't been calculated, Hammond said.

The scale wasn't used regularly until the early 1980s, said David Oppenheimer, a seismologist with the U.S. Geological Survey in Menlo Park, California. A magnitude from another scale can be calculated as a Richter scale measurement, he said, but doing so would be like turning a compact-disc recording of Beethoven into an old-fashioned 78-rpm monophonic record.

INDEX

—E—

Earl's lodge, 227
Earthquake Park, 193, 194, 197
  photograph, 194
earthquakes
  after, 250
  during, 249
  injuries, 247, 249
  largest, 265
  occurrence, 247
  preparedness, 245, 248, 256, 257, 260
East End Road, 41, 263
East High School, 209
East Hill Road, 7, 34
Easter Bake Sale, 75
Eaton, Millie, 155
Edens
  Brant, 76
  Dick, 75, 76, 79
  Velma, 75, 80
  editorial, 105
Egan, Bill, 167, 222, 227
Ekron, Shirley, 98, 99
Elks club, 36
Elmendorf Air Force Base, 181
Eskimo National Guard, 168
Eskimo Scouts, 172
Estill, Jack, 89

—F—

F.E.M.A., 246, 247
FAA
  Kenai, 156
Fairbanks, 13, 70, 72, 203
Fairview Ave., 45
Family Cafe, 49, 55, 57
Farnen, Larry, 67
Federal Building (Anchorage), 224
Federal Energy Management Administration, 246
Fifteenth Avenue, 42
Fifth Avenue, 156, 211
Formella
  Jim and Bernice, 155
Fort Belvoir, Virginia, 169

Fort Richardson, 183
Four Season Apartment Building, 224
Four Seasons Apartments
  photograph, 223
Fourth Avenue, 13, 14, 34, 145, 173, 211
  photograph, 215
Fox Island, 136

—G—

Gebhart, Clara, 231
Gerkin, Mary, 55
Girdwood, 34
Glenn Highway, 185
Glennallen, 185, 189
Glennallen Community Chapel, 189
Glennallen Power Plant, 186
Globaline, 260
Gnad
  Bruce, 41
  Harold S., 41
  John, 42
  Peter, 41
  Ruth, 41
Government Hill School, 219
  photograph, 219
Green Timbers, 46, 53
Greer
  Al, 39
  Jill, 39
Gregoire, Harry, 31
Griffin, Joy, 5
Gulkana, 186
Gusher Bar, 88

—H—

Haeussler, Peter, 255, 262
Halazone, 260
Halibut Cove, 63, 65
Hall, Frank, 156
Haltiner, Dick, 59, 89
ham radio operators, 9, 13, 58, 167
Hammond, Bob, 265
Hammond, Jay, 62
Hart, Walter, 157

Heady Hotel, 36
Heavilin, Bob, 256, 260
Hendricks
  Laura, 143
  Reggie, 143
Hewlett, Natalie, 62
Highway Department
  State of Alaska, 240
Hillside Apartments, 226
  photograph, 225
Hillstrand, Earl, 89, 227
Holiday Inn, 173
Hollis's Service Station, 55
Homer, 43, 45, 72
Homer airport, 53
Homer dock, 64
Homer Electric Association, 46, 68, 69, 86, 101
Homer harbor, 24, 64, 86, 104
Homer High School, 41
Homer Hospital, 39, 45
Homer Junior-Senior High School, 9
Homer News, 105
Homer Post Office, 39, 55
Homer Public Library, 75
Homer Spit, 21, 24, 58, 59, 64, 68, 69, 80, 82, 86, 99, 105, 227, 263
Homer Volunteer Fire Department, 256, 259
Horn, Loren, 156
Hoyt, Jr., Roy E.,, 155
Hummel, Jack, 155, 156
Hunt, David, 49
Hurricane Hazel, 187

—I—

IBM, 178
Idiak Baptist Mission, 119
Island Lake, 119

—J—

J.C. Penney's, 156, 172, 177, 211, 216, 220, 221, 224
  photograph, 214
J.C. Penney's, 233, 234
James, Pete, 156

INDEX

INDEX

Robert Earl, 137
Nelson, Hulda, 85
New Madrid, Missouri, 265
Nickolas, Jess, 156
Nikiski, 11, 13
Ninilchik, 27
North American plate, 255, 262
Northern Lights Boulevard, 193, 202
Nuka Bay, 83

—O—

O'Malia, Tom, 157
O'Malley (street), 178
Old Harbor, 209
Oppenheimer, David, 266

—P—

Pacific Northern Airlines, 170
Pacific plate, 255, 262
Panhandle Bar, 173
Parfait Shop, 33
Pate
    John, 35
    Margaret, 35
    Mike, 35
Patton, Andy, 237
Person, Julia A., 197
Petersen Bay, 65
Phillips
    Francis, 206
    Jane, 205
    Mary Lee, 205
    Susan, 205
Pierson, Miles, 156
Pillar Mt., 112, 113, 121
Pioneer Avenue, 57
Pioneer Hardware, 55
plates, tectonic, 255, 262
Platt, Betty, 31
Platt, Poopdeck, 153
Poole, Martin, 36
Poore
    Debbie, 149
    Lisa, 150
    Tracy, 150
Porpoise Room, 21, 22, 58, 59, 69, 77, 86, 91, 104

Port Lyons, 139
Portage House, 155, 157
Portland, Oregon, 77
Post Office Mall, 173
Presbyterian Hospital, 175
Price, Susan, 255, 259, 263, 265
Prince William Sound, 19
Propane, 261
Providence Hospital, 220
Public Health service, 23
Purcell, Robert, 256, 259, 263

—Q—

Quartz Creek
    landing strip, 156

—R—

railroad dock
    Seward, 19
Ram (fishing vessel), 64
Red Cross, 23, 37, 77, 135, 207
Red Mountain, 89
Resurrection Bay, 227
Rhode, Leo & Floris, 85
Rich, Joe, 221
Richter scale
    discussed, 265
Robinson, Anne B., 3
Romig (street), 171
Romig Junior High School, 219
Ronda
    Ann, 6
    Arlene, 5
    Don, 5, 41

—S—

Safeway stores, 214
Salty Dawg, 21, 82, 86, 90
Salvation Army, 207
San Francisco, 10, 181, 197, 203, 224, 265
Saturday Evening Post, 221
Sawyer, Colonel Kenneth T., 237

Sayer, Dr. Paul & Nancy, 85
Scenic Park, 175
Schmid, Bob, 153
Sealand Transportation Company, 81
Sears Roebuck, 211, 216, 220, 221
Seattle, 177, 203
Seldovia, 91
Selief (power scow), 15
Send International, 191
Seward, 15, 19, 20, 21, 34, 36, 52, 70, 72, 94, 147, 156, 207, 208, 218, 227, 229
Seward Harbor, 227
Seward Highway, 150
Sewell, Avery, 89, 91
Sewell, G.G., 59, 90, 91
Shelford
    Lee, 82
    Sunny, 90
    Tom, 80
Shohl residence, 195
Shumagin Islands, 265
Slagle, Lloyd, 215
SMALL BUSINESS ADMINISTRATION, 36
Smith, Dean, 156
Spenard, 170
Spenard Lake, 212
Spenard Road, 206
Spenard Safeway, 212
Spillers, Julian (Jit), 157
Spruce Cape (boat), 138
Spruce Cape (place), 139
Standard Oil tank farm, 81, 89, 91, 92, 104
    photograph, 81, 102
Stariski Creek, 27
Starr, Doctor, 228
Sterling Highway, 88, 150, 232
Sullivan, George, 62
Summit Lake, 156
Sunrise Inn, 156
Sunshine Mall, 173
Sven (baker, Valdez), 162

INDEX